FASCIST EUROPE RISING

THE REPRESSION AND RESURGENCE OF DEMOCRATIC NATIONS

Rodney Atkinson

BLOOMFIELD BOOKS
26 Meadow Lane
SUDBURY
Suffolk
ENGLAND CO10 2TD
Tel: Sudbury (01787) 376374

1

Published by:

Compuprint Publishing

1 Sands Road,
Swalwell
Newcastle upon Tyne NE16 3DJ

Copyright © 2001

Paperback £12 ISBN 09525110 4 5

This book is also available direct from the publisher at the
above address for £13 including postage

British Library Cataloguing in Publication Data.
A Catalogue record for this book is available from the
British Library.

Front cover: concept: Rodney Atkinson illustration: Chris Mabbot.

Printed by C.P. Print Limited, Newcastle upon Tyne

"The worst difficulties from which we suffer do not come from without, they come from within. They come from a peculiar type in our country who if they add something to its culture, take much from its strength. Our difficulties come from the mood of unwarrantable self-abasement into which we have been cast by a powerful section of our own intellectuals. They come from the acceptance of defeatist doctrines by a large proportion of our politicians. But what have they to offer but a vague internationalism, a squalid materialism and the promise of impossible Utopias?"

Winston Churchill, St George's Day 1933.

"We are at present working discreetly but with all our might to wrest this mysterious political force called sovereignty out of the clutches of the local nation states of the world. And all the time we are denying with our lips what we are doing with our hands."

Arnold Toynbee, Official in the British Foreign Office in both World wars, and from 1925 to 1955 Director of Studies at the Royal Institute of International Affairs, Chatham House, grandfather of the Europhile *Guardian* Journalist and BBC broadcaster, Polly Toynbee.

"Dr A. J. Toynbee, Professor at the University of London. Personally an obliging and skilful man."

SS General Walter Schellenberg, *Gestapo Handbook for the Invasion of Britain* 1940.

3

CONTENTS

PREFACE

During the 1930s when the seeds of an integrated Europe were being sown by an imperialist Germany, those in Britain who warned of that danger were called "Germanophobes". This author does not fear Germans, nor do I hate Germans — on the contrary — but I do know the history and motivations of the German State. I am aware of the corporatist nature of that State, the power of the German philosophical idea of the State and the correspondingly weak concept in German politics of the peaceful, trading nation and therefore of democratic nationhood in general. This was so well expressed by Friedrich Reck-Malleczewen (executed in a concentration camp in 1945) when he wrote in his *Diary of a Man in Despair*: "... in 1500 there was a German nation but no nationalism whereas today we have the reverse, nationalism and no nation."

I must emphasise that I do not believe that it is the German people who deserve censure for the historical and actual ambitions of the German State and its corporate sponsors. Germans have been taught since the end of the second world war that it was "German nationalism" which twice brought war to Europe and that therefore their embrace of something called "Europe" was a democratic ideal to bring reconciliation to their neighbours. But in fact it was not German nationalism but German supranational imperialism which brought Europe to war. But having sold the peaceful concept of "Europe" to their people the German state has in fact used that concept, and the flag and institutions of the European Union as a cloak for their nationalist ambitions and as a vehicle for the realisation of those ambitions.

I myself cannot blame Germans in general for this and I believe I am in a position to make this assertion on the grounds of my personal life-long involvement with German institutions, friends and students. At my 21st birthday party in Newcastle upon Tyne a sixth of the guests were German students. During my degree course I taught for a year at the Domgymnasium ("Cathedral Grammar School") in Fulda, at that time near the border with communist East Germany. My German honours degree included a distinction in spoken German. Through the film and folk clubs I founded when I was (for five years) a lecturer at the University of Mainz and through the extra-curricular English language courses I ran in England during the University holidays I believe I have done more than the typical "europhile" to promote friendship and understanding between the British and German peoples. I have been rewarded by the regular return to England of many of those former students, one of whom, inspired by the British folk songs he learned at Mainz, has continued to introduce English music to the choirs and ensembles he conducts in Germany.

A British newspaper reported some years ago a visit by Edward Heath to Germany where, seated at a dinner table he cut a lonely figure, unable to converse in the dominant language of that European Union which he had worked so hard to create. In this he resembles a large number of the europhile element in British politics whose belief in the Eurostate is based not on experience of or communication with those with whom they wish to combine in one economy, polity and State but rather on an ignorance and fear of the consequences of not joining them. By contrast most of the leading voices in the eurosceptic movement are experienced "continentalists" and linguists whose intimate knowledge of the cultures, languages and histories of one or more European nations leads them to recognise the unbridgeable, but rich and admirable, distinctions between them.

The longer one studies a people and a language other than one's own, the more one is aware of the very subtle but very great differences between that culture and one's own. But my experience of Germans of all ages is that they differ very little from the British people in one important respect — their rejection of the ambitions of their own political establishments to create a European Superstate. To that extent at least there will be reason even in Germany to welcome this book.

INTRODUCTION

Free people and nations develop a variety of constitutions, a variety of political systems and different patterns of social and economic behaviour. Totalitarian regimes are the same the world over, possessing as they do the same tools of seduction and oppression. As the constitution of the Danish people rightly asserts "It is by law you build the land" and it is through the debasement of the law of nations that imperialists conquer and fascists rule. No other regime in the history of the world has achieved so much imperial conquest by merely manipulating the law as has the so-called "European Union".

For centuries the historical bulwark against continental European tyranny has been Britain (and prior to 1603, England). The historical essence of British power has been the allegiance of the British people. The foundation of that allegiance has been in the historic freedoms under the law provided by parliament (against the arbitrary rule of the Monarch) and by individual legal freedoms enjoyed by the people (against the arbitrary rule of their law-makers). But all these freedoms and protections and most of the pillars of that great 800 year old constitution have been diminished or destroyed by the secret, parliament-bypassing machinations of a post war European hegemony in the disguise of the European Union.

The principal characteristic of this European Union, indeed the feature most lauded by its promoters, is its size. That size is equated by europhiles with power, or, for Tony Blair for instance, with "superpower". A leading Dutch politician said some years ago that the EU was so big, so complicated and so involved that it could not be undone. Romano Prodi, the President of the European Commission, stung by the rejection by the Irish of the Nice Treaty, said that the European idea was so great and the "only hope for the future" that "the difficulties are because Europe goes through a democratic process". And when this intoxicating "bigness" causes the predictable corruption and lack of accountability, as in the Common Agricultural Policy, the Common Fishing Policy, fair trade, crime, illegal immigration and much else then the resulting chaos is seen by the eurofederalist planners not as a crisis but as an opportunity to acquire more power at the centre. A classic recent case is the response by the former Marxist student radical and now German Interior Minister, Otto Schilly, to the riots in Genoa when he called for a European Riot Police with a European-wide database of "troublemakers" onto which he would immediately volunteer 13,000 names of Germans!

When a system's principal *raison d'être* is physical size and political power (like the European Union) then it will inevitably prove to be an alienating, anti-democratic force devoted at all costs to self-preservation. The size is the force and the power is the glory. Since the natural development of such powers is to disintegrate, ever more authoritarian force is exerted from the centre until sooner or later an explosion of social and political resentment breaks the entire edifice apart. Given the advanced state of such authoritarianism in the European Union even before it has completed its "project", the break up of Blair's European Superpower is inevitable.

Like all totalitarians the fanatical supporters of this new European empire have a dictionary full of euphemisms to tempt the unwary (see chapter 1) and a raft of propaganda slogans which they believe, by mind-numbing repetition, will move the masses. In the same chapter I describe six insidious techniques with which the European Union has undermined the free nations of Europe. Hitler rightly believed that success in politics came not from truth or rational argument but from finding a gut instinct, then a phrase which arouses that instinct and promotes your message and finally repetition in every medium month after month, year after year. The words chosen by the European Union have been the (totally undefined) "Europe", the touchy-feely "Community" and the breathtaking hypocrisy of "jobs at stake" (when the European Union means mass unemployment and the non-membership of Norway and Switzerland and the non-Euro status of Britain have brought full employment).

9

The ease and insouciance with which the new totalitarians lie soon allows them to use words which signify the exact opposite of their normal meaning. An excellent example is provided by Chris Patten the fanatical Europhile whose dismissal by British voters handed him far more power than election would have done (the Governorship of Hong Kong and now a European Commissioner). Patten says "opposition to the European Union is unpatriotic". He is joined in this Goebbelesque project of word bending by the "Britain in Europe Campaign" supported by Eurofederalists like the Conservative Kenneth Clarke the Liberal Democrat Charles Kennedy and of course the Blairite Labour Cabinet who claim to be "... the *patriotic* pro-European campaign. We believe that a strong role in Europe is in Britain's *national* interest." It was the greatest supporter of the destruction of the British constitution on the altar if the European Union, Tony Blair who said, *"We are a patriotic nation."*

Needless to say in the linguistic world, unlike the political, there is still a constitution and rule of law by which we can judge tyrants who would destroy our language as effectively as they have destroyed our democracy. That linguistic rule of law is laid down in dictionaries and, like laws defending individuals against the arbitrary rule of fascists, so the *Oxford English Dictionary* presents the real meaning of words:

"patriotic"
devoted to the wellbeing and interests of one's country

"nation"
a distinct people organized as a separate political state

But Britain is no longer, by treaty, by constitution, by political reality a fully-fledged "separate political state". Therefore it is not a country and therefore support for its status within the European Union cannot be "patriotic". The dictionary tells us therefore what ordinary people knew anyway — *that it cannot be in the national interest to abolish the nation.* But that is precisely the Orwellian intention of the Europhile manipulators of our language and our minds.

This book seeks to reveal the true intent of the creators of the new European Superpower and to dissect the propaganda which seeks to sweeten the bitter pill of the destruction of democratic nationhood. By strengthening the minds of "the sovereigns" (ie the people) of all nations against the eurofederalists' practised deceit, by quoting the nation-destroyers' unguarded admissions of their true aims and by providing in the final chapter a tool for the re-assertion of democracy 1 hope this book will aid the restoration of those free nations for which millions died in European wars during the 20th century.

Chapter 2 describes the first step to fascism — corporatism, that obnoxious mixture of authoritarian collectivism of left, right and centre which is so palatable to the bureaucrats, lawyers and petty functionaries on whom the democratic vacuum bestows such oppressive power. The chapter also describes (together with Appendix II) the grotesque propaganda machines of the European Union and the BBC. Chapter 3 details the true nature and intent of the creation of the Single European Currency, the Euro, the implications for democracy and (what remains) of the British constitution, the disastrous consequences for Germany of the Euro and European Union membership and how the United Kingdom, within the EU, is virtually trapped into joining the Euro. Chapter 4 describes the return of German Europe, the attempts to recreate Charlemagne's empire and the increasingly fascist nature of the European Union and indeed the British government under Blair. The chapter also describes the illegality of the NATO/EU war against the sovereign state of Yugoslavia, its break up into the same statelets created by Fascist powers in the 1940s, the break up of Czechoslovakia and Germany's use of the idea of "Europe" to reassert its influence over Eastern Europe in general. Finally the "achievements" of German Europe are summarised in an analysis of the threat posed by the new "Europe" to the United States.

In Chapter 5 I describe the use of the South Molton Declaration within the United Kingdom as a means of reasserting the sovereignty of the people and hence democratic nationhood throughout Europe. Finally Appendix II lists the individuals, or-

11

ganisations and corporations in Britain who have contributed most to the creation of the bureaucratic, corporatist Eurostate by bypassing the electoral, democratic and parliamentary institutions of our once free nation. The names of those who have conspired to undermine our nation and democracy must be permanently recorded, first so that they can be identified and countered and secondly so that they cannot reinvent themselves at some future date as "defenders" of everything they have in fact destroyed.

The true extent of the achievements of this evil and covert project is clear in the recent judgement by a stipendiary magistrate in the matter of a greengrocer in Sunderland who had weighed and sold produce in pounds and ounces, rather than in the weights and measures of the new imperial power — kilos and kilograms. Although it is not at all clear whether the basis for the defence in this case was wise, the fundamental dismissal by the stipendiary magistrate of the powers of the British Parliament are quite ruthless and in part even cynical.

The defence argued that the Government had brought in legislation to enforce the metric weighing and sale of produce via a 1994 order based on the 1972 European Communities Act. But subsequently the 1985 Weights and Measures Act, which permitted the use of imperial weights and measures overrode and impliedly repealed the 1972 Act. Therefore the Sunderland greengrocer was entitled to weigh and sell in pounds and ounces. This was in fact a weak defence on two grounds. Firstly the prosecution was in fact under the 1985 Act which despite permitting imperial weights and measures allowed the Secretary of State at any future date to vary the order and remove any particular weights and measures from the list. Secondly it is evident that the 1972 Act was not concerned with *particular* matters of governance but established an entirely new constitutional framework. In the words of the Honourable Sir John Laws, (quoted by the Sunderland Judge) the 1972 Act: "Falls to be treated as establishing a rule of construction for later statutes ..." Needless to say a matter of mere weights and measures could not be in that constitutional class.

Whatever the defence presented in this case, the prime significance of the judgement is in its brutal description of the constitutional destruction of the Houses of the British Parliament by that 1972 Act of Accession to the European Union. This comes as no surprise to those of us who argued with parliamentary candidates about the South Molton Declaration at the 2001 General Election (see chapter 5). We repeatedly pointed out to those who wished to retrieve sovereignty by piecemeal measures or by partial assertions of the "power" of the British Parliament that only the fundamental assertion of the sovereignty of the British people (for instance through the South Molton Declaration) could overcome the overriding "rule of construction".

The way in which a fascist regime can, by gradual, secretive means take over not only the constitution and laws of a free nation and the powers of its democratic parliament but also, insidiously, the very mind set of its people can be seen in the following extract from the Sunderland judgement:

> The Diceyian view of the illimitable sovereignty (of Parliament) offers a view expressed before the concept of a European Union: *Any Act of Parliament or any part of an Act of Parliament which makes a new law or repeals or modifies an existing law will be obeyed by the courts — there is no body of persons who can, under the English Constitution, make rules which override or derogate from an Act of Parliament or which will be enforced by the courts in contravention of an Act of Parliament.* In like vein Blackstone writes of "The omnipotence of parliament" and Sir Edward Cohen: *The power and jurisdiction of Parliament is so transcendent and absolute that it can not be confined.* However these are the writings of constitutional commentators of yesteryear. Time has moved inexorably onwards. Every law student of my generation lapped up these sayings with alacrity. It is true we believed they would stand the test of time, now they are only of interest from the historical perspective.

Thus speaks the bureaucrat, technician and lawyer of the passing of what he regards as "historical and non-binding parts" of

a constitution in which "times have moved inexorably on-
wards". In noting the "once seemingly immortal concept of the
sovereignty of parliament" the Sunderland judge has in fact described the passing away of democracy itself. For in the modern era of the universal franchise it is the people, not
parliament who are sovereign and the end of sovereignty *is* the
end of democracy.

Although it is not my contention that the judge was wrong in
his judgement of this case, it is his failure to grasp the essential
nature of a constitution and of a democracy which is typical of
the many functionaries who, uncontrolled by the modern pro-
fessional politician, both devised and now interpret the bureau-
cratic/administrative law which has secretly destroyed
democratic nations. This ignorance of the nature of a democratic constitution can be seen from his little homily:

> Constitutional law is not like a stagnant pond, never chang-
> ing. It is like a fresh running stream, constantly changing as
> it does to accommodate the surrounding land and the va-
> rying weather patterns, so it is with our constitution in order
> to meet the needs of the time and age in which we live.

A classic case of a little knowledge being a dangerous thing,
although such misinterpretations of a democratic constitution
are repeated *ad nauseam* by "leading" politicians. For the essence of a constitution is that it is not a political document but
a framework within which politics can change and "time moves
on" *without undermining the pillars* of the system the constitution prescribes. Secondly a *democratic* constitution, once it
abandons the sovereignty of the people, is no longer either
democratic nor a constitution — but that is precisely what the
evil, Edward Heath-inspired 1972 European Communities Act
did. The democratic representatives of the British people, behind their backs, without their knowledge or consent, usurped
the people's sovereignty and thereby the powers of their parliament — *acts which the constitution of the land did not permit.*

In a recent case, *Pepper v Hart*, the meaning of a law, where it
was a matter of contention, was adjudged to be that which

14

Government ministers indicated was their expressed intention when the law was passed. In the case of the 1972 European Act it was the Prime Minister Edward Heath who insisted in Parliament that the act did not involve "any loss of essential national sovereignty". The intention of Parliament therefore was diametrically opposite to the reality which ensued from that Act — as so clearly described by the Sunderland judge. If at the outset the will of Parliament did not concur with the (covert) intentions of the Prime Minister of the day, then it is no wonder that today a judge can swear allegiance to the Queen and simultaneously impose an alien constitution on the once free British people.

That mere administrators of the law can today dismiss with sublime indifference the pillars of the greatest parliamentary constitution in the world (which sporned scores of other constitutions, including that of the United States) shows how, by subterfuge and deceit, the British people have been deprived of their heritage, democracy and nationhood. I can conceive of no other term than "fascism" to describe the methods whereby this evil has come about and the anti-democratic and imperialist European powers which have carried out their historic project.

The British people will not rest until that evil has been expunged.

CHAPTER 1

THE FECKLESS DESCENT

"I have watched this famous island descending incontinently, fecklessly, the stairway which leads to a dark gulf. It is a fine broad stairway at the beginning but after a bit the carpet ends."
Winston Churchill

1. DOES BRITAIN STILL EXIST?

The EURO, the "Single European Currency", was launched on the 1st January 2000, although, in the now long tradition of European Union deception, the constituent currencies of the 11 countries which joined the EURO will still be in (apparent) circulation until 2002.

The EURO is not the "first step towards a United States of Europe"; it is the last step in the creation of a United States of Europe because it is the most important. Without its currency, central bank and control of overall spending decisions through the national Treasury no country can be said to be in charge of its own affairs and therefore its own government. In constitutional and democratic terms therefore that country is no longer a country but a province of another country — in this case the European Union. Other European Treaties may have curtailed most of the rights of European Union nations to govern themselves *but the abolition of national currencies contained in the 1992 Maastricht Treaty is not a matter of national control but of national existence.*

Long before the launch of the EURO the British constitution (like all the other constitutions of the nations of Europe which are members of the European Union) had been fatally undermined. The British parliament no longer governs Britain, the British courts no longer decide or interpret our law and decisions about who can cross our borders and vote in our elections no longer reside with the British Government.

The British people have lost their exclusively British passport (the one document which has in the past proved conclusive in the determination of treasonable conduct) and have become "citizens" of the European Community, with duties towards and taxable by the EU. The "Common Market" which Westminster approved in 1972 and the British electorate approved in 1975 never existed. The 1972 accession to the Treaty of Rome was a constitutional act, not an international agreement and the European Communities Act of that year destroyed the 800-year-old (written!) British constitution. The 1986 and 1992 European Treaties merely extended the aegis of the 1972 Act to ever more areas of policy making and ate ever deeper into the fabric of the British constitution. It is a myth that there is no written British constitution. It has been written down for nearly 800 years in statute and common law, but unlike other nations, we do not have a codified constitution with a Constitutional Court. Instead we have the supremacy of parliament — or rather we did have until Heath signed the Accession to the Treaty of Rome on the 22nd of January 1971.

Every day the European Commission in Brussels and the European Court of Justice in Strasbourg issue directives, regulations and court judgements which our democratic parliament has made itself powerless to resist and which outnumber and have more far reaching significance than Westminster's own activities.

Since 1971 the method chosen to destroy the British constitution (Treaty Law) had the same effect as Hitler's emergency powers from 1933 (introduced by German "centre parties" in 1930!) — the bypassing of parliament and the democratic process. Treaty law was used in 1972, 1986, 1992, 1997 (Amsterdam Treaty) and 2000 (Nice Treaty) illegally to destroy the British people's right to self-government.

There is no longer a British fishing industry there is no longer a British Agricultural industry and "ministers" with those responsibilities in the British "Government" are men of straw, whom it is pointless for the British electorate to try to influence. (Some 300,000 of those disenfranchised fishermen and farmers took to the streets of London because their democratic "representatives" were as powerless as they.)

The extension of Qualified Majority Voting within the European Union means that there is no area of policy (even areas where we in theory have a veto) which cannot become the subject of bargaining by European civil servants and ministers behind the backs of the British people. The British people and the free Nations of Europe have lost everything they fought two world wars to preserve — nationhood, self-government and democracy. *The three major political parties in Britain never mentioned any of this in any party manifesto and yet it has come to pass, behind the backs of the electorate and in contravention of every tenet and convention of a democratic constitution.*

Those who have brought the nations of Western Europe to their enslavement within the new Superstate knew that no electorate would ever approve of their plans to destroy the democratic constitutions of 15 countries. They knew that in a fair referendum the answer to any such proposal honestly expressed would be "No". They therefore only put the kind of anodyne questions to which they could (with a large amount of State propaganda and disinformation) obtain the answer "yes". When the Danish people gave a 51% "No" to the Maastricht Treaty they were told they had to vote again but when the French voted 51% "Yes" they were, needless to say, not required to reconsider!

It has always been a tactic of totalitarian regimes to use frequent plebiscites, suitably manipulated, to obtain a pseudo justification for their dictatorships. So it has been in the history of

18

the European Union. The most basic manipulations have always been 1. to accept 51% majorities to approve the kind of constitutional destruction which *within* most of the nations would have required two-thirds majorities and 2. to put the question in such a way as to ensure that the answer the political Establishments wanted would be "Yes" (The kind of psychological assessments done by politicians to study how they can get their own way despite the people's wishes have always shown that people prefer to say "Yes" rather than "No"). In other words a question like "Do you wish to remain a sovereign self governing country?" (to which few would answer "No") is never allowed, only "Do you wish to be part of a European Community?"

The long list of such euphemisms which Tory, Labour and Liberal parties have used to persuade the British people to surrender their constitution is a testament to the anti-democratic manipulation which has taken place. Anyone listening to the attitudes and track record of the former German Chancellor, Helmut Kohl in his crusade to abolish the nation states of western Europe on the altar of the "European" Union would quickly recognize in him the old Hitlerian "Fuehrerprinzip" (Leader Principle) which laid down that an efficient democracy consisted of the people voting for a leader and then doing what they were told.

This attitude, like so many of the legal principles and attitudes of the authoritarian Continental system, have now been either forced on the United Kingdom by European Union Treaties or eagerly taken up by Labour, Liberal and above all Tory politicians (the latter signed the three critical Treaties in 1972, 1986 and 1992). So instead of describing the Treaty of Rome which Prime Minister Edward Heath signed in 1972 as the constitution-destroying document it was, the British people were asked if they wanted to be part of a "Common Market" of free trading sovereign nations — and who could object to that? And when Geoffrey Howe and Douglas Hurd deceived Mrs. Thatcher about the "Single Market" legislation in 1986 they told her that if we signed up to it we could force other EU members to open up their markets to our goods and services (although why after 30 years of a supposed "common market" this had not been achieved was not explained!). But in fact the 1986 legislation, by introducing more than a dozen new areas of political and economic decision making to majority voting, was at that time the greatest single loss of democratic rights the British people and parliament had ever experienced. It was, needless to say, never widely debated either in the media or in Parliament. When John Major (who even today claims to reject the loss of the democratic rights which he long ago signed away!) sought to obtain approval for the Maastricht Treaty legislation in the House of Commons he asked the British people if they did not wish to be "at the heart of Europe" — a geographic and therefore political and economic impossibility if there ever was one! Indeed it was the minister in Konrad Adenauer's government of the 1950s, Hans Seebohm, who succinctly put the German view of "the heart of Europe":

> Germany is at the heart of Europe and the limbs must adapt themselves to the heart.

The Maastricht Treaty of 1992 was even more disastrous than the Single European legislation of 1986, (not least in the acceptance of the principle of the *acqis communautaire* which under the legal concept of the "occupied field" gave the European Union permanent rights to decide the law for all member states in any field in which they had already legislated). All these treaties were in fact doing no more than bringing ever more areas of national life under the control of that fundamental constitutional destruction when Britain acceded to the Rome Treaty in 1972 (in particular under Section 2 of Heath's European Act of that year).

The permanent damage done to the British parliament, constitution and nation by Edward Heath and his "Minister for Europe" Geoffrey Rippon cannot be overestimated. In his wilful lies to parliament and the British people (recently openly admitted) Edward Heath was guilty of the most heinous crime ever committed by a British Prime Minister — *not least because he was warned in detail in advance of the horrific constitutional and democratic consequences of what he intended doing.* It was his Lord Chancellor Lord Kilmuir who having been asked by Heath to study the constitutional implications of becoming a signatory to the Treaty of Rome replied that the proposed treaty:

> *would go far beyond the most extensive delegation of powers even in wartime that we have ever experienced. It is clear that the European Council of Ministers could make regulations that would be binding on us even against our wishes. It is the first step on the road that leads to the fully federated state ... I must emphasis that in my view the sur-render of sovereignty involved is serious ... these objections ought to be brought out into the open.*

But Heath had absolutely no intention of permitting an informed debate on the destruction of the British Constitution which accession to the Treaty of Rome would bring about. The House of Commons, (with few notable exceptions) was blissfully ignorant of the actual content of the treaties the government was signing and the meaning of the domestic legislation which put that treaty into force. Parliament was deliberately misled by a government which assured them that "there is no question of a loss of essential national sovereignty". In fact of course, while voting for an apparent "free association" or "common market of sovereign nations" MPs were in fact voting for their own democratic castration. For that 1972 European Act relegated the Parliament of the United Kingdom from a sovereign democratic institution to one subservient to the European Commission and the European Court of Justice. The principle of the superiority of European institutions was established by Edward Heath, although the actual political reality of that loss only became apparent over the next 30 years as, by ministerial agreement, by the judicial activities of the European Court and of course by treaties like Maastricht and Amsterdam that basic constitutional castration of 1972 was applied to ever more areas of our political, economic and social decision making.

The euphemisms came thick and fast as the years of secret constitutional destruction went by. The "Single European Market" was sold on the basis of its "market" to a British government which wished free and fair trade. But as massive state subsidies in France, Germany and Italy and the exclusion of 60% of the nations of Europe testified the Single European Market was neither European nor a market. But the critical word was "single" for this was the real intention of the legislation, not fair trade but a single economic entity. A single market is a contradiction in terms. Either you trade freely with most countries of the world or you seek to create a special group of countries which form a trade block within which trade is done on favourable terms. But nations outside that block are not part of that "market" and therefore they are effectively taxed by those inside. To no countries did this protectionism apply more perniciously than those countries of Europe (nearly 30 of them) which even today are outside this privileged and protectionist group calling itself the "European" Union. Of those 30 countries most are in Eastern Europe where nations which have just escaped from the clutches of the Soviet Union find that membership of the European Union would take away their hard won democratic national self government.

It is these poor former satellites of the Communist Soviet Union which now find they cannot sell their produce to their nearest neighbours in Europe because the "European Union", while claiming to trade freely within its own borders, has raised insuperable barriers to trade externally and can only accept, say, agricultural produce from Poland if Poland becomes part of the quota setting, price controlling, subsidised and state run system known as the European Union's Common Agricultural Policy. It is little wonder that economic disenchantment in the East is now combined (following the war against Yugoslavia) with a more aggressive approach towards the west and a more pugnacious attitude from Moscow.

But while the former eastern bloc nations cannot benefit from trade with the European Union there are apparently no constraints on west European countries taking over, for instance,

Polish farms or media companies or Czech and Slovak corporations. One way across the borders (Eastwards) is open, the other way (Westwards) is closed. The "treaties" signed between Germany and, for instance, Poland seek to impose the idea of equal rights to movement, jobs and property in the context of "European citizenship" which of course means the effective reclaiming of land and property rights by Germans expelled from the West of Poland after the war. (See Chapter 4, in particular *"Der Drang nach Osten"*.)

2. SIX TECHNIQUES TO DESTROY FREE NATIONS

There have been several devious techniques used by Eurofederalists to construct a United States of Europe on the corpses of once free nations. The two obvious methods of creating an anti-democratic European superstate — waging war and open, democratic discussion and approval — were of course out of the question. The former had failed on several occasions and the latter would not achieve the desired outcome.

THE FIRST TECHNIQUE has therefore been secrecy and deceit. The true aims of the Eurofederalists could never be revealed. This process is best summed up by two of its practitioners, the English historian Arnold Toynbee and the former French Foreign Minister Claude Cheysson. Toynbee said at an international gathering in Denmark (not, you will note, in England) in 1931:

> *We are at present working discreetly but with all our might to wrest this mysterious political force called sovereignty out of the hands of the local nation states of the world. And all the time we are denying with our lips what we are doing with our hands.*

Cheysson said a few years ago:

> *We could never have constructed Europe by democratic means.*

THE SECOND TECHNIQUE has been to create the impression of "inevitability" with the concomitant technique of

23

the "deadline method". The "European train" (which metaphor has the advantage of suggesting movement along a proscribed track of a vehicle which if you don't get on board "in time" you will "miss") has its treaties which are "inevitable" and those treaties are full of the words "irrevocable" and "irreversible". The train must move from one "stage" or station to another and like a timetable Kohl, Mitterand and their ilk always referred to the next deadline as being for instance "the March summit in Copenhagen" or the "December summit in Paris" by which time "the next stage" must be agreed — especially if there was in fact no agreement in sight!

THE THIRD TECHNIQUE has arisen conveniently out of the fact that 9, 12 or as at present 15 member states could never agree a clear and specific wording for any treaty. As a result broad principles are written down but cannot be applied directly to everyday political, social and economic cases. Therefore the European Court of Justice (which admits its task is to promote the integration of the states of the European Union) is called upon (daily!) to interpret the treaties and therefore to make law in the interests of the new central state ("the country called Europe" as some in the European Commission have called it) and against the sovereign interests of the constituent nations.

THE FOURTH TECHNIQUE is the "pragmatic interest group" technique which is part of the "salami slicing" approach. Having set out to deceive national electorates about their true constitutional intentions the Eurofederalists have been anxious to take short, *pragmatic* steps in the process of overriding the rights of European nation states. For instance it is now vital to their cause that the EURO be seen as a purely economic step, of convenience to trade, businessmen and bankers and saving holidaymakers the burden of changing their money within the new Euro-zone. When the CBI was asked by the Eurofederalists (and when the CBI asked its members) whether they supported the "Single Market" they were asked to consider it "purely from a business point of view". The National Farmers Union asked its members if they would like to do

24

business in the EURO "purely from an agricultural point of view". The Trade Unions were asked whether they wanted European provisions on working time or parental leave or board room consultation "purely from a Trade Union point of view" — and how could they say no? But in fact the Single Market, the EURO and the Social Chapter were not political agreements between co-operating nations *but the constitutional structures of the new European Superstate*. These organisations representing businesses and workers were not, as they believed, signing up to industrial and employment policies but to the ("irrevocable and irreversible") right of the European Union, and not their own parliament, to make all such decisions in future.

THE FIFTH TECHNIQUE has been never to discuss the next anti-democratic step in the destruction of national democracies until that stage had already effectively been achieved. In other words in 1972 Heath's European Act (which enacted the provisions of Britain's accession to the Treaty of Rome) completely destroyed the constitutional right of the Westminster parliament to pass laws for the British people and of the British courts to interpret and judge them — although all under the disguise of an apparently harmless treaty to form "an essentially economic" "Common Market". When in 1986 what little discussion there was concentrated on the "loss of British parliamentary control" the fundamental question of loss of democratic sovereignty had in fact already been decided in 1972.

Similarly when the Maastricht Treaty discussion of 1992/1993 introduced majority voting to even more areas of political decision-making, the *principle* of adding ever more areas of majority voting (and hence loss of self government) had already been accepted in 1986. When Prime Minister Blair signed the Amsterdam Treaty in 1997 there was minimum discussion of the rights of British subjects not to be exposed to a foreign legal jurisdiction. But this principle had already been put into statute form in the 1989 Extradition Act and, through treaty law, in the Maastricht process.

On the same principle the present discussion of the abolition of the Pound, HM Treasury and the Bank of England (in favour of the EURO and the Frankfurt Central Bank) is based on the assumption that the UK has not yet signed up to European Monetary Union. But in fact that is exactly what the Maastricht Treaty was all about and the UK's "opt out" is at best ambiguous. First the UK has accepted stages one and two of European monetary union as laid out in the Maastricht Treaty and has only opted out of stage three — i.e. the introduction of the EURO and the abolition of the Pound. If we compare the Danish opt out (which is very brief and very clear — and given even more clarity by the recent NO vote by the Danes!) with the British opt out we see that in our case bad drafting of the opt out and opt in clauses make it unclear whether we need to positively opt in or just passively do nothing and find ourselves part of the EURO by not saying no! Secondly the legal requirements of the Single Market legislation of 1986 could always be used by the constitutionally activist "European Court of Justice" to force the UK — or any other member of the European Union — to adopt the EURO on the grounds that "a single market means a single currency". Indeed the words "Single Market", having no other logical meaning, was always intended to pave the way for a single currency but like every other piece of Eurostate planning the true intention had to be either disguised or blatantly (and repeatedly) denied.

THE SIXTH TECHNIQUE is perhaps the most insidious of all — gradually inserting into every aspect of a nation's life the insignia of the imperial power (the stars of the European Union flag). Already this very unpopular flag or logo can be seen on some car licence plates, on flags flown from public buildings, on flags flown by some of the biggest corporations (like Forte Hotels) and on some driving licences. More will come — quietly, secretly, without any fuss or democratic approval. One day, when the British people and, who knows perhaps even their so called "democratic representatives" awaken and talk of the rights of the British nation, the conquering power will say "The British nation? What is that? The nation is called Europe

— look around you, the flag of Europe is everywhere. Oh of course there are a few Union Jacks, but they are being replaced by the St Andrews Cross and the flag of St George, but of course *they* only depict regional allegiances, like Bavaria or Aquitaine, not self-governing nations. The Queen? But she became a citizen of the European Union in 1992 at Maastricht, as your then Home Secretary Kenneth Clarke confirmed at the time. The Parliament at Westminster? Oh no that is merely an assembly where English representatives are responsible for regional government. It has no real sovereign powers." For now the conquering power *does* recognise the word sovereignty — its own! And so the conquest of a sleeping people is complete.

Ever since the incorporation of Hitler's "regional principle" into the structures of the European Union and the recreation of petty nationalisms (Croatia, Wales, Slovakia, Scotland) for "regional development" purposes and as a method of breaking up non-racial nations, the unity and power of the United Kingdom has been under threat. The response of some English political activists has been to counter that threat by promoting an "English Parliament". I hope that the above demonstrates clearly how dangerous that policy would be. For only the British Parliament has been sovereign and only the Union flag and of course the Pound Sterling represent that sovereignty. The newly created "Welsh Assembly" has no historical basis, the "Scottish Parliament" has not been sovereign since 1707 and neither is sovereign today. An English Parliament would inevitably join them in their powerlessness and become a regional government for an English province of the European Superstate. Indeed by describing the Scottish assembly as a "Parliament" the British are inviting the new masters in Brussels to justify the same lack of sovereignty even to the British, never mind the English, "Parliament".

It is interesting to note what might have happened if the EURO had *risen* against the Pound — and the other national currencies which did not sign up to the EURO — instead of collapsing ignominiously against all the major currencies of the world. It was made clear as the "Stability Pact" was being drawn up

(designed to "co-ordinate" the economic and exchange rate relations between those EU member countries within the EURO
and those outside) that "unfair competition" from countries
whose currencies were weak against the great EURO would not
be permitted to "undercut" producers inside the Euro-zone.
This was despite the free trading terms of the Single Market
legislation. However the reverse situation has occurred — there
is an enormous trade advantage for those countries *inside* the
collapsing EURO who can now undercut producers *outside* the
Euro (but within the Single Market). Strangely there is no sug-
gestion that the latter can take action against the "unfair competition" of Euro-zone members. This demonstrates once again
the essentially corporatist and politicised nature of the "builders
of the European Union". Laws are passed and regulations applied but then the whims of politicians and arbitrary majorities
decide to suspend or ignore those rules.

It is typical of an enterprise, which seeks power and control
rather than freedom and democracy as its principle aims that
vagueness, far from being a disadvantage, is a great ally in
manipulating public opinion. But when this — as in the European Union — leads even professionals and experts in economic and financial affairs to fail to define their terms then the
dangers are obvious. I debated, alongside that most principled
of democratic representatives, Christopher Gill MP against a
pair of MEPs the value of British membership of the EU (we
turned a two-thirds majority against us at the outset into a two-
thirds majority for us at the end of the debate). By way of
introduction to the debate a representative of the Bank of England gave a "factual presentation" during which many statistics
concerning "Europe" were displayed. I asked him if he could
give us the Bank of England's definition of "Europe". I asked
whether he meant the 42 countries of Europe, the 15 members
of the European Union or the (then) 11 members of the EURO.
He rummaged round in his tables, notes and speech and had to
admit he could not say what definition of Europe had been
used to compile his "information". Not long before an article
had appeared under the name of a leading member of the Bank

of England in which the writer referred repeatedly to a "common currency" the idea of which (proposed by Nigel Lawson as a European currency parallel to national currencies) had long since been abandoned in favour of the *Single* European Currency which would abolish and therefore replace all the national currencies.

3. SOVEREIGNTY, POWER AND THE NATIONAL INTEREST

Within the various strategies used by the Europhile to trap the unwary into a federal European State there are a number of principal themes. The most insidious is the argument that each step in our constitutional destruction is taken "in the national interest". The process of secretive steps over a period of 30 years has entangled ever more areas of our nations' political, social and economic life *within the fundamental constitutional destruction of Heath's 1972 Act.* As the trap began to close, politicians could say that since "x" and "y" are already facts then "z" is a logical step without which "the national interest" could be severely compromised. Gradually these "next steps" turned from being (apparent) agreements to co-operate and increase trade with other nations (hence the use of international treaties) into the imposition of a legal system "to enforce fair trade". Then that body of law — originally sold to the parliaments and peoples of Europe as "purely economic" — was extended to social and environmental affairs. The next step was to extend that body of law to questions of "free movement of people", *even though of course the whole purpose of the free movement of international capital is to make the movement of people (and the social dislocation and cultural alienation that entails) largely unnecessary.* It is not surprising that as the State has taken over ever more areas of economic decision-making (taxing capital, preventing its free movement and applying exchange controls) international mass-migrations have increased. Indeed many migrants are escaping government persecution as well as seeking a better economic life.

The European Union, far from being a combination of sovereign States committed to free and fair trade has been a bulwark of protectionism and state controls, protecting state and private businesses within its borders and applying (especially to non EU European countries) protectionist tariffs. This — plus large subsidies to multinational corporations to set up within the EU — has led to an artificial boost to business within the EU's borders and impoverishment and attempted mass migration from outside. It is typical of a superstate, which has undemocratically stamped its control over other nations within its borders, that it should by its collectivist subsidies, and controls, deprive poorer nations of their resources.

But let us return to the inexorable logic of the step-by-step entrapment of the formerly sovereign and free European nations by the European Union and its superstate fanatics. As the body of EU law (the *acqis communautaire*, which overrides all national law, all national parliamentary rights and all national constitutions) grew after each "logical and pragmatic" step of EU integration each radical constitutional step in that process could be described as being part of the whole. In other words if an electorate rejected the idea of becoming "European citizens" then they were told that they would also be rejecting free trade. If they rejected an EU passport this would make taking holidays in Europe more difficult. If they rejected the Single European Market (which was a blatantly political construction) they were rejecting the common market (which *seemed* at least to be an economic idea). If they reject the abolition of their national currencies for the "single currency" then they are "rejecting the single market". All these steps were then described as "being in the national interest" of each member country. But by the end of this process what they are in effect saying is it must be "in the national interest to abolish the nation" — a complete illogicality. But by then of course the reality of national sovereignty has virtually disappeared anyway and only an "empty shell", as one German minister called it, remains.

One of the more grotesque (or insidious) arguments of the eurofanatic is the claim that national sovereignty is about "exerting power in the world" and it is an "old fashioned concept". Sovereignty, it is claimed, is irrelevant today because the nation "cannot decide its own destiny" and must therefore combine to form a "powerful block" which alone has "the power to exert influence in the world". At a public meeting in Newcastle upon Tyne the author debated with a Conservative MP who was formerly a *Financial Times* journalist (and thereby steeped in multinational corporatism) and an agriculture minister (and therefore administrator of the EU's Common Agricultural Policy) who suddenly burst into aggressive voice saying "it's power, Europe is about power — that's what we want". His name was David Curry MP and his little outburst was sufficient to turn even more of the audience away from his views (our side won the debate with about 90% of the vote).

But sovereignty — i.e. national democratic self-governance — has nothing to do with power. Some of the largest states in the world have no sovereign power (i.e. California) while the smallest states (like Norway, Switzerland) are sovereign, self-governing nations. Sovereignty does not entail the power of a nation to dictate to others or even fix its own success, merely the power to define its borders, citizenship and the rights of citizens, govern itself through its own parliament and accept responsibility for its business, financial and trading decisions. It may make good decisions in which case it will tend to get richer or it may make bad decisions in which case it will tend to get poorer. In the latter case it is then up to its own parliament to make different decisions and it is up to the electorate to change those who govern them. The sum total of all these economic, social and political decisions is reflected in the external trading position, the country's earnings and the confidence of external investors, all of which are reflected in the nation's currency. That currency moves up and down to reflect reality and it is those movements to which individuals, families, communities, companies and governments themselves react. As soon as the currency is "fixed" or government controlled or, (as with the EURO) abolished then that vital reflection of a living, organic, self regulating, democratic entity (the nation) and all the emancipated and free decisions of people within it disappear. It can never be in the national interest to abolish the nation's sovereignty, the most potent sign of which is its currency.

If the EURO had been merely an attempt to make financial, economic and business intercourse between nations easier — a kind of international currency which paralleled national currencies like the "Special Drawing Rights" instituted by the IMF or the embryo internet currencies — then one could view the enterprise as an emancipation of the nations rather than a control over them. Indeed this is what the "common currency" proposed by the British under Nigel Lawson's Chancellorship would have been, but it was of course rejected. Why? *Because the European Union had already put into place all the ingredients for the destruction of its member nations and a common currency would have frustrated that aim.* Only the national currencies remained to be destroyed to conclude the covert but breathtakingly arrogant project to create the European Superstate.

Just as the first step of those nations to free themselves from the iron grip of the Soviet Union was to re-create their own parliaments, budget, Treasury and currency, so the opposite process occurred in the 1940s as the Nazis marched in to conquer and subdue other nations. Between 1940 and 1945 the Nazi project to "integrate Europe" involved a single market and the beginnings of a single currency. The local currencies were fixed against the Reichsmark and a clearing system was established in Berlin which would have inevitably developed into a central bank with the Reichsmark (or the same under some other name — perhaps the "Euro") circulating in all conquered nations. This is not surprising for to control a currency is to control the country for just as a currency reflects the whole economic and democratic life of a country so it also contains all the assets and liabilities of that country. Most do not speak of "Scottish oil" because all Scottish oil is an asset of the Pound Sterling. We do not speak of California fishing grounds because all the wealth in those grounds is an asset of the US Dollar. As discussed below in more detail, the step which really creates the new German European Superstate is the creation of the State's currency — the Euro. After that step everything else (in theory) falls neatly into place.

CHAPTER 2

THE EUROPEAN UNION – THE ENEMY OF FREE NATIONS

1. CORPORATISM — THE FIRST STEP TO FASCISM

In July 1997 the German Parliament passed a resolution which referred to the final achievement of a post war peace settlement in Europe. Britons and Americans had assumed this had been achieved in 1945 — but this is not the view of that German political class (supported partly out of fear, partly out of hubris by France) which has constructed today's European Union by destroying those democratic nations re-established by the Allies after the war.

"German Europe", in the form of the "European" Union, representing a small minority of European states is already turning back the clock and re-establishing that economic and political corporatism and collectivism which presaged European and world-wide conflict in the 1930s.

Furthermore the democratic destruction which has taken place has been aided by the United States which, like Churchill, uses the term "a united Europe" in the sense of European nations being united in friendship — not in a single state. But the corporatist, protectionist and authoritarian nature of west European politics has a different vision and that vision is as dangerous today as it was in the 1930s.

It is also unfortunate that US industrial corporations are aiding the aims of the European Union in the name of mere business convenience. General Motors sees the abolition of the Pound, the Bank of England and the remains of sovereign government in the United Kingdom as a price worth paying for their factories' profitability. This is chillingly reminiscent of the critical support for the Nazi economy and war machine by large US multinationals in the 1930s. The extent to which the Hitlerian project for Europe has been reproduced by transatlantic corporatism since 1972 was nowhere better demonstrated than in October 1997 when a senior executive of General Motors demanded that the British abolish the Pound and the Bank of England in favour of the Single European Currency or else the company would close its production in the United Kingdom.

General Motors has a record of political and economic support for European oppression. In 1936 the US ambassador in Berlin complained to Roosevelt about that company's "enormous business here, they complicate things and add to our war dangers".[1] By 1936 General Motors subsidiary Opel was one of the two leading producers of tanks for the Nazi war machine[2] and in 1935 the US War Department protested to the company about its transfer of ethyl lead technology which was so critical in military aircraft.[3]

It is precisely such *corporatist* power (the term means the power of all "bodies" be they companies, trade unions or other collectives bent on political power) combined with State control, which we fought two world wars to defeat. Now we are threatened by companies who have been guests in Britain for many decades, playing with our 800-year-old constitution as they would with a car production line. As the President of the Norwegian parliament said of the Nazi take-over in 1940: "What stupefied the Norwegians was how men with whom one had had intimate business relations, who had been cordially welcomed in one's home were in fact agents of destruction."[4] As my book *Europe's Full Circle* demonstrated, the same threats to our nations and democracies now return in the ambitions of multinational corporations. The American collaboration with the Nazi regime (intentional or not) was of a far higher order than that of which the Swiss have been accused — and, unlike Switzerland, the USA was not surrounded by two all-conquering fascist powers.

It is doubly unfortunate that NATO, 80% of whose effectiveness is due to American weaponry and funding, is being shamelessly used as a battering ram to extend the power of the European Union further east and south. The recent German-inspired break up of Yugoslavia is a classic case. From their unilateral recognition of Croatia in 1990 to their arming of the terrorist KLA in order to provoke Serbia the German led European Union has harnessed NATO to achieve Germany's historical aims (see below Chapter 4).

2. INTERNAL DECEIT AND EXTERNAL APPEASEMENT

The European Union today reflects in the actions of multi- national corporations and in the words of its leading politicians and (a minority of) trade unionists exactly the same ideology and prejudices which drove Hitler's Germany, Mussolini's Italy and collaborators in France during the 1940s. I have set out below a brief extract from Chapter 11 of my book *Europe's Full Circle*, which demonstrates this remarkable symmetry between the two periods.

When Edward Heath signed the Treaty of Rome and took the United Kingdom into the "European Common Market" his Government assured the British people that they were entering a common market of sovereign (i.e. self-governing) nations. "It is this simple economic concept" as the Government said at the time "that is at the heart of the Community. The impact of Community law is by definition confined to essentially economic matters. There is no question of eroding essential national sovereignty."

Now that the British parliament, democracy and 800 year old constitution have been fatally undermined it is not unusual to hear those who, like Edward Heath, planned that destruction, admitting, for the first time, their long held aims. But some were more open earlier. Raymond Barre the former Prime Minister of France said, "I never understood why public opinion about European ideas should be taken into account."

A group of British parliamentarians formed a so called "Design for Europe Committee" in 1947 under the chairmanship of Peter Thorneycroft, the leading Conservative Politician and later Chairman of the Tory Party (1975-1981). Their anti-democratic and secret intent was spelt out:

> No government dependent on a democratic vote could possibly agree in advance to the sacrifices which any adequate plan must involve. The people must be led slowly and unconsciously into the abandonment of their defences.

And in the modern era it was the Liberal Democrat party leader Paddy Ashdown — reflecting the praise heaped on the last great "integrator" of Europe, Adolf Hitler by the Liberals' Earl Lloyd George (1863-1945) and Lord Lothian (1882-1940) in the 1930s — who said that:

> I do not believe that the nation state is anything other than a recent historical invention. I do not believe it will always remain.

In fact, thanks to the covert, undemocratic machinations of multi-national corporations, the Brussels bureaucracy and a small coterie of Westminster politicians (from all three main parties), our nation and its democracy have indeed been largely destroyed. For today even historical protections under Magna Carta and *habeas corpus* have been overridden by the rights of other European countries to have British citizens automatically arrested and extradited from the United Kingdom.

This process was well summarised by the words of a former Tory MEP, Bill Newton Dunn:

> When ministers go to Brussels they leave their democratic baggage behind them.

Mr Newton Dunn found a more natural home for his anti-democratic ideas in the party of Prime Minister Tony Blair. Enemies of democracy within and without our borders have cleverly constructed this evil process. The important thing to remember about signing agreements with the European Union is not to trust any promise or indeed any word which seems to protect national or democratic interests for those words will be used not to communicate but to deceive. British (and indeed French) politicians for example were deceived by what *seemed to be* a clear protection of their national interests — the national veto. But that veto right is now so restricted that no British government has ever used it in case there is a cost to be paid in areas where there is majority voting. The logic is well summarised in the following comments by a European Union official:

> If Britain wants to be at the heart of Europe there is a price to be paid. That price comes in the form of (the end of its) budget rebate and we need new movement on tax. If the British do not give in on these areas there will have to be concessions elsewhere — for instance with a big cut in EU regional aid to Ulster or Scotland.

This not unusual tirade by a mere civil "servant" is made more ludicrous by the fact that there is of course no such thing as European Union "aid". Britain pays — even with its rebate — billions of Pounds more to the European Union than it receives. Indeed it was in Ulster (Northern Ireland) that the true political nature of the European Union "project" was again revealed. The European Commission, having lent money to a company there pointed out that unless that company flew the European Union flag they were unlikely to receive any "help" again! So here is another lesson for the free nations of Europe — do not trust European Union civil servants to be fair and objective administrators. They are not. They are the front line of German Europe's imperialism and the Goebbels-like propaganda machine which operates in all European Union countries. An official European Commission document lists 100 areas in which Brussels wants to "improve Brussels input into education and training".

3. THE PROPAGANDA MACHINE OF THE EUROPEAN COMMISSION

There are no lengths to which the unelected European Commission will not go to expose our most vulnerable citizens (schoolchildren) to their propaganda — and this in an area (education) from which the European Union's own treaties (never mind successive British Education Acts) officially exclude it.

During the 1999 European Parliament elections an organisation called "The Charlemagne Group of Companies" spent millions of pounds "informing" the electorate about the glories of the European Union — even though at least three of the parties standing at those elections opposed the UK's membership of the Union. This demonstrates the urgent requirement to amend the Representation of the People Acts.

Not long ago the EU official responsible for a "New Approach to Audio Visual" was trying to put Pro EU propaganda into popular sitcoms like "Highlander" in the UK, "Alle Zusammen" in Germany and "Hors Limite" in France. *The Times* quoted the official as saying "We are talking about product placement, or even idea placement ... sitcoms are the best way to get the message across." The proffered subsidy for including the "idea placements" was 5% of production costs. There has always been a ban on political advertising on British television but the EU propaganda machine managed, for a time, to advertise by "sponsoring" old films on Channel Four.

The propaganda of the European Commission's cartoon story for children the "Strawberry Ice cream War" was so disgraceful that it had to be withdrawn but that has not prevented the circulation in our schools (accompanied by so called "Europe days") of an EU propaganda pack called "Euroquest" which parades as a "quiz" about "Europe" (but is of course purely about the wonders of the European Union.) If anyone doubts the insidious nature of the "European Project" in the United Kingdom then these EU attempts to infiltrate British education and entertainment should be more than enough proof of the nature of that project. A detailed description of the propaganda war being waged in British schools by the European Union is contained in Appendix 2 at the end of this book.

Perhaps the most insidious of all the attempts by the European Union to extinguish the once free, self governing nations of Europe is the so-called "regional principle". The device was a favourite of European fascism in the 1940s so that national governments were bypassed and regional committees reported directly to Berlin. In the European Union this system has gone one step further — the very borders of the nation states are being extinguished.

The Leader of Kent County Council is now President of a Euro Region comprising Kent, Nord Pas de Calais, Flanders, Wallonia and Brussels. The Chairman will be French or Belgian. The EU authorities are attempting the same in Sussex, linking East Sussex to a "partnership" with Seine Maritime and Somme with a French "project manager" (how forensic and managerial these political take-overs sound) installed in Lewes County Hall in East Sussex.

At a recent international conference organised by myself in Oxford, Jan Myrdal, the distinguished Swedish Social Democrat and intellectual (whose parents, uniquely in the world were both Nobel Prize winners) noted that "In 1943 the Oberburgermeister of Munich spoke of how strong municipal self government was in Germany — the municipalities as the cornerstone of society etc. This is the way they organised it — the only thing was that there were no elections."

Today in the EU there are scores of new funding bodies for urban development, for academic research, for small businesses whose main aim is not to help businesses but to destroy national organisations by promoting Pan European structures and Brussels control. The most insidious is the town-twinning programme where a suggested oath of loyalty to the European Union was proposed and caused much anger in Britain. The instruction in the official European Union document was:

> Whatever version (of the oath) is eventually used must make clear that European unification is the prime aim of and reason for the twinning.

This political corruption of all the democratic and parliamentary virtues to which the British people are accustomed has been accompanied (as one might expect) by a massive economic corruption at the very heart of the European institutions. The annual loss of up to £6,000m by fraud and mismanagement in the European Commission is proving a persistent drain on national resources.

The truly obnoxious nature of that corruption can be seen in the treatment of the individuals who have had the courage to expose it. Paul van Buitenen, the European Audit Commission member who leaked the details was taken by an employee of the European Commission to view some guns! — very subtle. Bernard Connolly who was head of the Commission's EURO department and who wrote *The Rotten Heart of Europe* was excluded from the commission buildings, his picture was put up in public corridors, he was ordered — illegally — not to leave the country, his phone was tapped, his wife was followed and received many nuisance telephone calls and his house was broken into.

When Britain joined Heath's "Common Market" we were the third richest country in Europe. Today we are the fourteenth richest (by GDP per head although we are now the fourth biggest economy in the world). All the countries which remained in EFTA and did not join the EEC, became richer as we became poorer. Today the richest countries in Europe are Norway and Switzerland, which are not, have never been and do not wish to be in the European Union.

In return for a total net budget contribution of £30,000m we have joined a club with which we have accumulated a manufacturing trade deficit of over £150,000m since 1972. For such an economic disaster the British people — without knowing it — sacrificed their historical rights to self-government and protection under the 800-year-old British constitution. In the annals of British self-government this association with "Europe" will be seen as by far the most disastrous series of decisions in our 1,000 year history. As a leading Eurocrat said recently, the creation of the EURO meant that:

> It will be the first time we have achieved such a result without arms.

Democrats who fought two bitter wars to preserve the democratic self-governance of European nations may well ask what has happened. Once they have grasped what they have lost they will see there is only one solution. We must withdraw from the constitution-destroying structures of the European Union and return to the common market of self governing nations for which the British people voted in 1975 — and in which there are to be found today the richest and the freest nations of Europe!

The threat of the new, undemocratic and assertive power bloc, which the USA has helped to construct, is now becoming evident in Washington (see below Chapter 4 section 10). The refusal to obey WTO judgements, the attempt to fix EURO exchange rates against the Dollar, the attempts to impose European regulations and values on non-European countries, the dumping of surplus agricultural produce on the third world and now even the courting of Fidel Castro who sees the EURO as a weapon against the Dollar. And this is not to mention the carnage wreaked in Yugoslavia by the interventions of Germany and the European Union into which US troops are now being drawn (on the side of their historical fascist enemies and against their historical allies) because their politicians did not read their history books. Is it not time that the American nation awoke to the complete unwinding of the post war settlement for which so many of the youth of their nation died?

1. Edgar B Nixon ed., *Franklin D. Roosevelt and Foreign Affairs*, Vol. III, Cambridge, Mass., 1969
2. Professor Anthony Sutton, *Wall Street and the Rise of Hitler*, Bloomfield Books, 1976, p. 31.

3. United States Congress, Senate Hearings before a Subcommittee on Military Affairs, Scientific and technical mobilisation, 78th Congress First Session, S.702, GPO 1944.

4. Winston Churchill, *The History of the Second World War*, Vol. 1, p. 546.

THIS IS AN EXTENDED AND UPDATED VERSION OF THE TABLE INCLUDED IN CHAPTER 11 OF THE BOOK EUROPE'S FULL CIRCLE

HITLER'S EUROPE	TODAY'S EUROPE
1936: Chamberlain took over from Baldwin, Halifax from Eden and Vansittart was sent to the Lords.	1990: Major, Clarke and Hurd took over from Thatcher, Ridley and Lawson.
1938: Munich.	1992: Maastricht.
"The world belongs to the man with guts. God helps him." Adolf Hitler in Joachim Fest, Hitler: Eine Biographie, Frankfurt, 1973, p. 683.	"Might is right in politics and war." Helmut Kohl, 1996. "What we want is a man of sufficient stature to hold the allegiance of all the people and to drag us out of the economic morass in which we are sinking. Send us such a man and be he god or the devil we will receive him." Paul Henri Spaak, former Belgian Prime Minister, President of the Consultative Assembly of the Council of Europe 1949-1951.
In his youth Hitler used to rub out Germany's borders in his school atlas.	As a young man Kohl got into trouble with the authorities for pulling down

border markings on the French-German border.

"The Germans alone can really organise Europe ... Today we are practically the only power on the European mainland with a capacity for leadership. The Fuehrer is convinced that the Reich will be the master of all Europe." *The Goebbels Diaries 1942-1943*, New York, 1948, p. 357.

"Look at Europe — what does it consist of? Britain? — aloof. France? — politically unstable. Italy? — economically unstable. And Benelux doesn't count. What does Europe therefore consist of? — Germany." Chancellor Konrad Adenauer, quoted by Henry Brandon in his book *The Retreat of American Power*.

Hitler said Czechoslovakia must in all be allied with Germany. He compared Czechs with "people who asked when the train would arrive at Potsdam. They could not be made to understand that this was quite impossible, because the train did not go there because the points were set that way. In Czechoslovakia they were also on the wrong train." Documents on German Foreign Policy 1919-1945. From the Archives of the German Foreign Office (Washington DC 1949) Series D no 158, p. 191, quoted in Gordon A. Craig, *Germany 1866-1945*, p. 708.

"Missing the European train." "We cannot go the speed of the slowest ship in the convoy." Helmut Kohl

"Germany is the locomotive of the European train" Helmut Kohl

"The Czech-German Treaty is ... also a setting of the points for future cooperation between our peoples." Helmut Kohl 1992

"Liberalism has been and still is the major source of the Community's weakness." French Text book on the European Union, 1994, quoted in Laughland, *The Tainted Source*, p. 145.

"Without France Europe will never equip itself with a single currency — more than ever the indispensable instrument with which to counterbalance the imperialism of the dollar." *Le Figaro*, 18th July 1997.

(The take-over of Elf by Total/Fina will make an oil company which is) "protected from any Take-over attempt by an Anglo-Saxon or American." Dominique Strauss-Kahn, French Finance Minister, July 1999.

The French Government is bound to surrender on demand all German subjects designated by the Government of the Reich who are in France or in the French possessions ... Franco German Armistice Agreement 1940, Article 19.

All "European citizens" may at any time, without presentation in court of any prime facie evidence be arrested and taken to Germany for trial. But Germany has exempted itself from extraditing Germans on the same basis. European Conventions on Extradition and (for the UK) 1989 Extradition Act.

"I wasn't allowed access to European Commission buildings, they posted mug-shots of me at the entrances. I was told totally illegally — not to leave Brussels without permission. My phone was tapped, my wife was follow-ed and she was bothered with nuisance phone calls. When I was away from home the house was entered at night. It was rather an unpleasant time — more like Moscow than new Europe." Bernard Connolly, sacked former Head of the European Commission's Department in charge of the European Currency.

Paul van Buitenen, a senior member of the European Commission's Audit Commission (which every year reports Euro-fraud of up to £6billion) reported his findings (and the failure of the Commission to act against fraud) to the European Parliament. Van Buitenen was taken by a European Commission official to view pistols and automatic weapons in the Commission's main building

"Germanic democracy (is) characterised by election of a leader and his obligation fully to assume responsibility for his actions. In it there is no majority vote on individual questions but only the decision of an individual." Hitler, *Mein Kampf*, Hutchinson, 1974, p. 83.

On 24th March 1932 the Reichstag passed the Enabling Bill which allowed Hitler to draft and enact legislation without parliamentary approval.

in Brussels. He regarded it as a threat and a warning!

"The era of true representative democracy is drawing to a close." Peter Mandelson MP, Minister Without Portfolio, April 1998

"European Policy has been conducted by a very small number of people — Kohl, Mitterand, Delors, two or three ministers; its a very small circle where decisions are taken and then ratified *a posteriori*, with regrets about the democratic deficit." Hubert Vedrine, chief adviser and negotiator to Mitterand at Maastricht (later Foreign Minister).

"Those who take a position against Maastricht will no longer have the right to engage in politics." Jacques Delors, January 1999

"My words may shock you but I declare that many of the great steps in the construction of Europe would not have been taken had we first had to hold a referendum." French Minister Claude Cheysson.

"Germany is no longer a law based state." Professor Albrecht Schachtschneider, University of Nuremberg, April 1998.

Dutch Reporter: "More than half the Dutch people want to keep the Guilder." Klaus Kinkel: "Then politicians should have the courage to take decisions if necessary against the will of the people." Reporter: "Excuse me?" Kinkel: "With the consent of Parliament of course." *NRC Handelsblad*, 31 January 1998.

"Today to make a common market without a common government is rather like putting the cart before the horse. It will be found that you cannot really organise a common economic system

"Why do the 15 EU states still need 15 foreign ministries and 15 diplomatic services? Europe would be stronger if it spoke to the outside world with a single voice. Why do we still need

without a common government." Sir Oswald Mosley, Leader, British Union of Fascists, in his book *Mosley Right or Wrong*.

"In 1500 there was a German nation but no nationalism, whereas today when our eyes are supposed to light up at 'Made in Germany' we have the reverse, nationalism and no nation." Friedrich Reck-Malleczewen, 1937, *Diary of a Man in Despair*, Audiogrove, 1995.

"Our people have been sold into the hands of international world capital. Do you want this to go on forever? Then vote for the capitalist parties." Nazi Party leaflet, 1930s.

"All effective propaganda must be limited to a few points and harp on these in slogans until the last member of the public understands what you want him to understand by your slogan." Adolf Hitler, *Mein Kampf*, Hutchinson, 1934, p. 164.

individual national armies? In Europe one army is enough." Hans Eichel, German Finance Minister.

"What does Europe therefore consist of? — Germany." Konrad Adenauer.

"The future will belong to the Germans when we build the house of Europe." Helmut Kohl, 1995.

Deputy leader of the CDU parliamentary party, Heiner Geissler, claimed on record that capitalism was no better than communism and lambasted "speculation profits" on the stock market. *Wall Street Journal*, 28/4/1998.

"It is judicious to act where resistance is weakest" (to pro EU propaganda). European Commission, de Clerq Report 1993.

"To the architect of the New World Order, the protector of justice, our leader Adolf Hitler, as a token of gratitude and loyalty from the Croatian People, Dr Ante Pavelic, Zagreb, 2nd April 1941.

"Danke, Deutschland." Croatian pop song, 1991.

"Your actions played a significant role in our political struggle." Ante Pavelic, Croatian Fascist leader, speech to Catholic Action, 21 June 1941.

"Genocide is a natural phenomenon, in harmony with the societal and mythological divine nature ... it is not only permitted, it is recommended, even commanded by the Almighty." Franjo Tudjman, former President of Croatia, in *Wastelands of Historical Reality*, 1989.

German Secret Service under Franz Neuhausen active in Yugoslavia throughout 1930s plotting the country's break up.

German Intelligence Service under Klaus Kinkel (Foreign Minister under Kohl) from 1981 starts intensive campaign to undermine Yugoslavia. E. Schmidt-Eenboom, *Der Schattenkrieger*, Econ Verlag, Dusseldorf 1997

1940s Yugoslavia: The papal legate in Croatia, Mgr Marcone, openly blessed the Ustashe and publicly gave the fascist salute.

On 5th October 1998 the Pope makes the former Cardinal Stepinac (1898-1962) of Croatia a saint.

51

In an official document dated May 8th 1944 His Eminence Archbishop Stepinac, head of the Catholic Hierarchy in fascist Croatia informed the Holy Father that to date "244,000 Orthodox Serbs have been converted to the Church of God". (FORCED CONVERSIONS) A. Manhattan, *The Vatican's Holocaust*, USA, 1986.

"Kurt Waldheim (awarded Croatia's highest honour in the 1940s) is usually the only guest at the fund raiser for Friends of the Waffen SS." *The Observer Magazine*, 19.8.1988.

1994 Waldheim receives a Knighthood from the Vatican

In 1940s Yugoslavia the Nazis broke up the country into many racial and religious statelets. The German Waffen SS divisions were organised ethnically — Handzar — the Bosnian Muslims, Kama — the Croats, Skenderbeg — the Albanians.

The first attempt to recreate a unit called "Handzar Division" was in Sisak, Croatia in the early 1990s.

More recently a Handzar division surfaced under the operational control of the Bosnian Government. One of its duties was to guard President Isetbegovic.

Now we do possess a European symbol that belongs to all nations equally. This is the Crown of the Holy Roman Empire which

embodies the tradition of Charlemagne the ruler of a united occident. It should therefore be considered whether the European head of State as the protector of European law and justice should not also become the guardian of the symbol which more than any other represents the sovereignty of the European Community."
Otto von Habsburg MEP, *Pan Europa.*

"The Anglo Saxon economic system the classic national economy is dead." Nazi Professor Heinrich Hunke 1941.

"The Nation State is increasingly losing its ability to stimulate growth, safeguard employment and allocate tax revenue, making it increasingly difficult for it to guarantee the foundations of its own legitimacy."
Professor Manfred Dammeyer, President of the EU's Committee of the Regions, Eisenstadt, Austria, 21/10/1998.

The Nazis' Regional Principle for the Government of Europe, in "Die Europaische Wirtschafts Gemeinschaft", Berlin

Paper by the European Union's Committee of the Regions: "Implementation of EU policy on Regions and Local Authorities": "The Union is no longer an association of Regions and Municipalities. The

Establishment of the COR is the ultimate recognition of that. Regions and towns play a crucial role in the ongoing process of European Union development."

"Radio wardens monitored compliance, one was forbidden to move from one's desk in an office until the broadcast had finished." *The Third Reich*, Michael Burleigh, Macmillan, 2000, p. 206.

"We are talking about product placement even idea placement — although there are similarities. Sitcoms are the best way to get the message across because they are set against the background of a particular reality. We just have to broaden into a European one. The Commission would insist on vetting scripts to make sure there were no inaccuracies. We are not insisting the Commission or the European Union be mentioned" (for their 5% subsidy). Santiago Herrero-Villa, official in the European Commission responsible for the department "NEW APPROACH TO AUDIO-VISUAL".

Max Amann, EHER VERLAG, bought the *Frankfurter Zeitung* and much of the Catholic Press. Ended up with 82% of German newspapers.

Large German purchases of Czech and Polish press and media, 1990s.

We do not have the feeling that we are an inferior race. Some worthless pack that can be kicked around ... we are a great Volk which only once forgot itself." Adolf Hitler June 1934, Gena.

"Germany has every interest in considering itself a great power in Europe (which must have) a foreign policy of fully acknowledged self interest." NATO "served to Protect Germany but also as a Protection against Germany ... this concept no longer has value." German Chancellor Gerhard Schroder, *German Unions Monthly Review*, September 1999.

"Only the Reich with its slippery historical frontiers remained truly sovereign with a depleted number of lesser nations in planetary orbit around its sun." *The Third Reich*, Michael Burleigh, p. 428.

"Vast tracts of Poland were simply incorporated into the Reich ... although the Poles soon discovered that Germans were keener to acquire industry than people." *The Third Reich,* p. 434.

"The German Parliament, in accordance with the treaty agreements with the states of middle and eastern Europe and most recently with the ratification of the German-Polish and German-Czech 'Neighbour treaties' has emphasised that in the process of the acceptance of our eastern neighbours into the EU ands NATO basic European freedoms must of course be equally applied without condition to all citizens in the old and new member states, including the German refugees." July 1998, Motion passed by the German Federal Parliament.

"We must foster as many such individual groups as possible i.e. (apart from the Poles and Jews) the Ukrainians, White Russians, Goraks, Lemkes, Kashubians. If there are any more ethnic splinter groups to be found then these too." Himmler, quoted in *The Third Reich,* p. 442.

Germany and The European Union recreated petty nationalist and religious statelets in Slovakia, Slovenia, Croatia and Albanian Kosovo and encourage the same in Scotland and Wales.

Many Jews survive today "thanks to the Circumstances that they were forced Labourers and not directly killed by the SS. Germans are tired of philosemitic over compensation in the media and sterile grief rituals of politicians." 2000, Professor Lutz Niethammer, Historical Adviser to the German Chancellor Schroeder.

"The Jews should consider whether they would have behaved heroically if they had not been victims of the persecution." 1998, Klaus von Dohnanyi, Former Mayor of Hamburg.

Between 1939 and 1941 500,000 ethnic Germans, under the programme "Home to the Reich" were "repatriated" from the Baltic, Bessarabia, Bukovina and Volhynia to Germany and to

During the late 1980s and early 1990s Helmut Kohl's government "bought" from the former Soviet Union the "Germans" of Kazakhstan who had been taken there by Catherine the Great but who the newly conquered territories of the Reich. "Sentimental guff regarding people whose connections with 20th century Germany were tenuous as blood rejoined blood and heart spoke to heart." *The Third Reich*, p. 448.

"I was looking through my collection of 'Dags Posten' the pro-Nazi culture daily for the educated. Friday 5th March 1943 had a spread on page 5, 'municipal self-government is strong in Germany', an interesting lecture in the Swedish German Society by Reichs-leiter Feiler, the Oberburge-meister in Munich and he was speaking of the German municipal system — you know the whole thing sounded very beautiful — the only thing is that there were no elections. On the one hand these municipal bodies needed no sanction from above but they had advisory bodies, so-called 'Ratsherren' to guarantee popular municipal policies and after-wards there was a supper and dance — this is subsidiarity." Jan Myrdal, Oxford Lecture, 31st October 1998.

by the end of the twentieth century no longer spoke German and who today in Germany are seen as Russians. Their only link was blood.

German Europe's "regional policy" has created the petty nationalist states of Scotland and Wales, but replaced England with eight regions each to be ruled by an "Assembly" composed of councillors (one each from District Councils) but who were of course never elected to serve on any "regional assembly" and includes members of unions and charities — also not elected. Each district has subscribed funds to the Assembly which will be responsible to Brussels through the equally unelected Committee of the Regions. Each region has set up an office in Brussels.

"People's Welfare" took over gradually the free charities and voluntary groups. A new national steering committee, under the guidance of a leading Nazi included the main religious charities. *The Third Reich*, Burleigh, p. 215.

The Political Parties, Elections and Referendums Act 2000 enacted by the Blair Government regulates and controls the registration, funding and spending not only of political parties but of any group engaging in politics. They all come under the "Electoral Commission". The power of the State now controls the democracy which was established to challenge and control the power of the State!

"An Easter card of 1942 showed a mother hen with *Europe, your Mother* written on her breast." John Laughland, *The Tainted Source*, p. 49-50.

In 1993 the European Commission used the slogan *Mother Europe must protect her children*. John Laughland, *The Tainted Source*, p. 50

The Federation of British Industry (forerunner of today's CBI) was concluding agreements with Nazi industrialists as late as March 1939 in Dusseldorf (after the Nuremberg race laws, the concentration Camps, imprisonment of thousands of political Prisoners, the Kristallnacht attack on the Jews and the invasion of Czechoslovakia).

"A random survey of businesses would be the ultimate gauge of firms attitudes to UK membership of EMU. Complications might arise in reconciling survey results with the existing CBI position if the outcome turned out not to be pro Euro." CBI memo April 1999

4. THE EURO-PROPAGANDA OF THE BBC — THE 1997 GENERAL ELECTION

For those who recall the behaviour of the BBC in the 1930s and its promotion of the government's policy of appeasing Hitler, it will come as no surprise that that organisation has engaged in a similar policy on the subject of Britain's absorption into the new Euro-state. Indeed given the exact reproduction of the institutions and philosophy of the Nazis 1941 plans for a "European Economic Community" (and similar anti-democratic methods of imposing it upon free nations) the BBC's political manipulations are entirely predictable. Not that the BBC is alone in this new appeasement since (just as in the 1930s) all three major political parties have been seduced into the destruction of their nation, parliament and democracy by a cunning and evil system which since the end of the Second World war has sought the re-creation of the aims of German Imperialism and continental fascism. Since the 1970s continental politicians found in the British political class the kind of appeasement and historical and political ignorance for which they had sought in vain since 1940. In the BBC they have found today the same fertile ground for their ideas as they found during the 1930s in Tories like Lord Beaverbrook (1879-1964) and Sir Samuel Hoare (1880-1959), Socialists like Ramsay MacDonald (1866-1937) and Lord Allen of Hurtwood (1889-1939) and above all Liberals like Lord Lothian (1882-1960) and Lloyd George.

Shortly after the 1997 general election I wrote to every one of the BBC's governors setting out the following complaints about the BBC's coverage of that election. I received not one reply from the Governors, all of whom are appointed — and paid — to represent the interests of the British public. It is of course that very public which (whether they watch and listen to its programmes or not) pay their licence fee to the BBC.

I set out here the items of complaint. What must be borne in mind is that we are dealing here not with just an average political discussion between politicians about social, economic or financial matters but about the entire democratic constitution of the United Kingdom. "Europe" is not a political issue, as its opponents on the left, right and centre demonstrate. Rather "Europe" challenges the very right of our country to exist and the power of our parliament to govern us — in other words it is a constitutional issue.

BBC journalists have never even grasped the rudiments of something they habitually call "Europe". They have not defined as "Europe" the 47 nations which make up the continent and therefore never allow that the so-called "European Union" consists of only 15 countries. They cannot let it be known that the richest countries in Europe — Norway and Switzerland are not, never have been, nor want to be members of the European Union. They dare not identify those present centres of resistance to "German Europe" (Britain, Serbia, Denmark, Norway, Switzerland) since they coincide exactly with the centres of resistance to fascist Europe in the 1930s and 1940s. They dare not itemise the enormous economic and budgetary cost of Britain's membership nor the true constitutional loss that has taken place. When it comes to the subject of "Europe" the BBC is at best all at sea and at worst engaged in a deliberate attempt to censor the truth. Indeed the promotion of the European Union's cause within the United Kingdom even leads the BBC to interview on a regular basis EU civil servants like Santer, Kinnock, Patten and Brittan. They would never dream of interviewing civil servants in Britain about what they were planning to instruct our government to do. Brittan and Kinnock were of course driven out of British politics by, respectively, a forced resignation over the Westland affair and repeated failure at the ballot box.

Throughout the 1997 general election therefore the following characterised the BBC's coverage of the "European" issue:

1. The discussion of the Social Chapter was conducted by all major parties and by BBC journalists in terms of whether certain social, employment and industrial relations policies were desirable or not. But this is not and never was the point of the Maastricht Treaty's Social Chapter — which Tony Blair signed

after the election. The Social Chapter was a constitutional document which handed over "irrevocably and irreversibly" the right to decide these matters to the European Union. Our political parties (and in particular the Labour Party founded for just such a purpose) will have no power to decide social, industrial relations and employment policies in the future. Not once was the discussion directed to this vital aspect of the "Social Chapter" by BBC journalists.

2. The discussion of the European Single Currency rarely if ever went beyond the standard euphemism to the essence of what this would mean — the abolition of the Pound, the Bank of England, the shared acceptance of all the pension, budget and national debts of the other member states, the pooling of (i.e. loss of sovereignty over) all our natural resources and massive increases in taxes to pay for "social cohesion". Since there is no example of a sovereign state without its own currency, it would mean the end of the United Kingdom and the final relegation of the once sovereign Westminster parliament to a regional assembly. Needless to say there was also no discussion of the massive regional, financial and social costs of disruption from the mass mobility of Labour which a single currency would require.

3. The discussion of the imposition of VAT on those goods and services so far exempt never once covered the fact that this was no longer a matter for the British government but a European Union responsibility. We have resisted imposition of VAT on food, children's clothes, house purchase etc only because of a temporary exemption from the EU's "harmonisation" directives. And yet BBC reporters allowed the Labour and Conservative Parties to do battle on VAT without mention of this constitutional loss (and therefore the irrelevance of their petty squabble!)

4. During the election VAT on fuel was of particular interest to the Labour Party and the electorate. But the BBC never discussed the fact that although the Labour Party opposed VAT on fuel in our own parliament their acceptance of the power of the

European Union meant they no longer had the power to abolish it — merely reduce it to 5%. Here was a case which revealed the impotence of a British government — because they could not act as a sovereign power and yet the issue (indeed the only issue in a democracy) was not discussed. Indeed if the VAT rate on domestic fuel had been raised to 17.5% by the previous Conservative government (only prevented by defeat in our parliament) the Labour government could by law not have reduced it below 15%. In the event Gordon Brown had to go to Brussels and ask if he could reduce the VAT rate on fuel to 5%. This was granted although, as the unelected Brussels bureaucrat said, the reduction was "against the spirit" of the EU VAT regulations. (EU regulations cannot be overturned by the British parliament!)

5. The BBC often mentioned Britain's opt out of the single currency as if we were the only country to have opted out. In fact Denmark had an official opt out and Germany had taken an unofficial opt out. In addition Austria, Ireland (because they believed at the time that they could not proceed without the UK) Sweden and Finland had also believed they could decide not to enter a Single Currency. Greece had at the time ruled out joining. Therefore Britain was never "isolated", as the modish phrase has it, on the opt-out. Either through abysmal ignorance of the various treaties and continental government positions, or in a deliberate attempt to mislead, the BBC never raised these facts for discussion.

6. The BBC gave much prominence to corporate executives from Unilever and Toyota who warned that not abolishing the Pound and the Bank of England (i.e. rejecting the EURO) would affect their investment in jobs in Britain. But no mention was made whatsoever of the exact opposite (and far more logical) statements by spokesmen from Honda, Nissan and the Association of Japanese Bankers in London. Nor did the BBC report Toyota's apparent subsequent about-turn when they said that staying out of the Single Currency could "boost the British economy". Some views accord with the BBC's political stance and prejudices, some do not. We know which get the coverage!

7. When Scots and Welsh devolution and independence were discussed during the election, BBC journalists did not point out that their independence movements are seeking the return of a sovereignty which largely no longer exists — since, thanks to the European treaties, there is little national sovereignty left in Westminster to "devolve". As the constitution of the United Kingdom was largely destroyed between 1972 and 1997 the BBC never mentioned the term "constitutional" at all. Suddenly when there was talk of devolving certain decisions to Scotland and Wales the rediscovered "constitution" becomes the subject of political discussion.

8. During the run up to the election the Labour Party leader dropped his party's proposal to give part time workers the same rights as full time workers. But this area of policy making had already been claimed by the European Union and will either be imposed on the UK under "Health and Safety" provisions or — now that Labour has signed the Social Chapter — become the responsibility of the European Union, not the British government. This aspect of the issue was not discussed.

9. Before the election the Labour Party had been found guilty in the British courts of unfairly discriminating against men in their women-only candidates lists. The Labour Party wished to change the law so that it could in future so discriminate. But in fact the European Union had already made such discrimination illegal and the German Christian Democrat party had had to reverse a similar policy. Yet again the BBC never raised these points of critical constitutional importance and joined the Labour Party in its pathetic ignorance of matters "European".

10. There was much discussion before and during the election of the Labour Party's "missing £1.5billion" in their budget calculations, of burgeoning government debt and severe constraints on expenditure. There was however one massive item of expenditure which dwarfed all other potential savings in the attempts to reduce debts. Strangely BBC journalists not once brought it up throughout the election — the completely unchallenged expenditure of £8,000m per annum which was then the

UK's budget contribution to the European Union. Similarly this disgraceful waste of taxpayers money never once featured in discussions of the shortage of funds for the NHS or the Education system.

11. Despite much airtime being devoted to discussion of the NHS, one issue was never raised on BBC programmes — the extent to which the European Union — by allowing "free movement of European citizens" across our borders and their right to obtain free NHS treatment — depletes NHS resources. There was also no discussion of the extremely dangerous re-naming of 150 of the most widely prescribed British drugs — ordered by the European Union and over which our Health "Ministers" had no control whatsoever. Normally the BMA representative has ready access to BBC studios — but not when the problem concerns "Europe"!

12. Throughout the election (and for years before) BBC programmes on the British fishing industry hardly mentioned the fact that there was no such thing as a British fishing industry — only a European Union fishing industry which makes our own "Fisheries Minister" largely redundant.

Although it is of course standard hypocrisy for a British MP to claim at election time that he can decide matters on behalf of the British voter and then kow-tow to his masters in the European Union, it should be the task of BBC journalists to expose this hypocrisy.

Our politicians' complete ignorance of the constitutional power of the European Union to override our democratic institutions is no excuse for equal ignorance on the part of BBC journalists. Most BBC journalists are not conspiring to cover up these matters, but they are simply (and dangerously) ignorant of what has happened to our constitutional rights. The way in which the BBC distorted the debate on Europe at the 1997 general election will, when its history is written, be ranked with the worst aspects of 1930s appeasement.

During the BBC's election night presentation following the count for the European parliament elections in June 1999, it was only towards the end of the programme that the UK Independence Party was mentioned — despite achieving three seats and nearly 8% of the vote nation-wide (the fourth largest party). On the other hand the BBC's own creation (principally through excessive exposure on Radio 4's Today Programme over several months prior to the election) the "Pro Euro Conservative Party", having been humiliated by its paltry vote, was given even more time after its political massacre than the UK Independence Party after its success.

A public sector broadcasting institution, funded by every television owner in the country, can only justify its privileged, state-protected position if it is accepted as a "public good" (i.e. that which only the State can provide). This it can only achieve if it does not take sides and gives fair airtime to all political points of view. This the BBC has conspicuously failed to do, partly because of the abysmal quality of some of its journalists and partly because the BBC has for decades cultivated a left wing "social democratic" bias — from which a broad section of political opinion (business, conservatives, libertarians, socialists and communists) have suffered persistent discrimination. In this case, of course, it is all political persuasions and even the democratic sovereignty of the nation itself which have suffered from the failure to analyse and describe the greatest threat to the United Kingdom since 1939.

Either the BBC must re-establish some semblance of objective journalism or a decision not to renew its Royal Charter cannot be long postponed. The very least we can expect from a democratic government — itself the result of competing political parties — is some competition in "public service" broadcasting.

CHAPTER 3

THE EURO – WHAT IT REALLY MEANS

1. THE PAST RECORD OF FIXING EXCHANGE RATES

There were three attempts at monetary union in Europe (uniting under one currency) in the 19th century — all failed. In 1987 the Tory Government tried to fix the Pound to the Deutschmark — this failed but not before causing an inflationary boom, the consequences of which still debilitate British citizens today. In 1992 the European Exchange Rate Mechanism (ERM) broke up completely, but not before instigating the longest recession since the 1930s. The two major international attempts to fix exchange rates — the Gold Standard in the 1920s (which led to the depression) and the fixed exchange rates agreed at Bretton Woods in the 1940s also broke up, as even politicians gradually realised that no one can fix any economic relationship without destroying the whole basis of the free and dynamic economy which relies on *spontaneous changes* in those relationships. The Euro (or Single European Currency) however is even more dangerous than these historical failures to control exchange rates since it is part of an "irrevocable" plan to create a superstate with one economy, one central bank, one government etc.

Perhaps the shortest monetary union of all time was that between the Czechs and the Slovaks after Czechoslovakia broke up in 1992. They tried to maintain a single currency between the two now sovereign states. They rapidly found that the management of a single currency was impossible between two democratic sovereign governments — even of two states which had together constituted one nation for over 70 years (with a break during the war when the Nazis split the country into two, just as "German Europe" has once again achieved today!)

Just as in the 1930s British appeasers of European Fascism tried to convince the British people that their nation was in terminal decline and that therefore an accommodation with Hitler would be advantageous so in the modern era those who are trying to build a United States of Europe, have tried similar tactics. In fact, despite our decline since joining the EEC in 1972, during the 1990s (because the United Kingdom opted out of Europe's social chapter (up to 1997) and the economic straightjackets of the Exchange Rate Mechanism and the EURO) Britons enjoyed an unprecedented period of economic growth. While other EU countries suffered years of mass unemployment, huge debts and (up to 1998) little growth, Britain flourished. British industrial workers became the richest in the EU and while the other countries had 6 years of stagnation and unemployment the British enjoyed economic growth and ever lower unemployment. Even today, after two years of modest economic growth in the European Union, unemployment in the UK is between one half and one third of the levels in France, Germany, Italy and Spain and in August 2001 reached a 26 year low.

2. WHAT THE SINGLE CURRENCY MEANS

The abolition of the Pound would not "merely" mean there would be no British control over the economy, interest rates or the exchange rate, *there would be no such thing* as the British economy, British interest rates or a British exchange rate. Therefore the British parliament — as befits a regional assembly — would have no economic control whatsoever over our economy. Economic policy would be controlled by Brussels (just as, now, Yorkshire's and Scotland's economic policy is decided in London).

The EURO, even before it was launched, proved to be a very weak currency. Even in anticipation of the EURO, the Deutschmark fell by about 30% against the Pound and the Dollar between 1992 and 1999. Since its launch the Euro (and hence all its member currencies) has fallen a further 15% against the Pound and 25% against the US Dollar. A weak currency will seek to protect itself. Having the powers to influence the EURO exchange rate the European Central Bank could, acting on a majority vote, impose exchange controls on the United Kingdom (or any other member state) thus preventing investment abroad. (Maastricht Treaty Article 73f) and under Article 73 g:

> The Council may take the necessary urgent measures on the movement of capital and on payments as regards the third countries concerned.

If the UK should abolish the Pound then it will become effectively a local authority within the new country called "Europe". Just as local authorities within the UK could be "rate capped" by the British Government so the Maastricht Treaty allows the UK to be fined if it does not meet borrowing, spending and inflation targets set by the new Government in Brussels. The idea that a country, which is so weak that it cannot meet economic targets, can then be fined is ludicrous but demonstrates clearly the intended "local authority" status of the UK within the European Union.

It is illegal under the Maastricht Treaty for the British Government or any British minister to even try to influence the governors of the European Central Bank. No matter how high unemployment rose no politician could complain to the European Central Bank, which has complete and unchallengeable power. Even Gordon Brown, the first Chancellor of the Exchequer since the war to give the Bank of England complete independence to set interest rates, has on occasion tried to influence the Bank to lower interest rates.

Despite no Conservative election manifesto ever having mentioned the abolition of the currencies of the EU and the possible abolition of the Pound, Douglas Hurd, the then Foreign Secretary signed the Maastricht Treaty on Economic and Monetary Union which said just that. Indeed, the so-called "opt out" of the United Kingdom from the Single European Currency is so unclear and ambiguous it is possible for Britain to be forced against its will into the EURO. Having left office, Douglas, now Lord, Hurd said: "I have never been an advocate of the Single European Currency."

German politicians, claiming as always that the European Union was designed to counter "dangerous nationalism" insisted that the European Central Bank should be based in Frankfurt. Indeed it was a German Finance Minister who said that "Either the European Central Bank comes to Frankfurt or the Euro will not get off the ground". The European Single Currency is "managed" by the unelected bureaucrats of the Frankfurt Bank. But to do so they will need to have detailed information about money supply, inflation and economic activity and the control of Euro bank note printing *in every EMU country*. In addition the ECB will have to trust each participating country not to print too many Euros! Given the trustworthiness of the process so far this is an extraordinary risk. The Board of the European Central Bank in Frankfurt has decided not to publish its minutes or voting record or even its inflation forecasts — all taken for granted in the United Kingdom and the United States. The ECB's guidelines — as we enter a period of potentially crippling deflation — contain a ceiling but no floor for inflation. In other words they could not respond to a massive deflationary *fall* in prices and the extremely high unemployment that might cause. *There is of course no convergence criterion for unemployment levels.*

The utter contempt with which the once free nations of Europe will be treated by bankers in a single European Currency was well illustrated by Otmar Issing an executive member of the European Central Bank board in an article in *The Financial Times* (where else — see below!) of 22nd September 1998: "National considerations must not play a role with the ECB even when conditions in one country differ markedly from the Euro-area average." In other words if peripheral nations like Italy, Portugal or the UK have very high unemployment, or high inflation nothing will be done for them, since only the core of the system matters. We can be sure that there will be even less willingness in Germany and France to pay massively higher taxes to provide "regional" subsidies to the United Kingdom, Italy or Ireland — although funds may be forthcoming in return for political obedience to the Euro-integrationists' will!

Since the British parliament and government would have no control over what would be no more than a "regional economy", they could in no way influence demand, interest rates, mortgage costs or economic activity. The present limited independence of the Bank of England can be removed by the decision of a British government but the *permanent* constitutional independence of the European Central Bank (which at present controls the entire Euro-zone countries and would control the UK should we decide to abolish the Pound) is completely out of the British government's control. After centuries of conflict between the House of Lords and the House of Commons over which controls money, the controversy would be resolved by control passing to Brussels and Frankfurt. Britain would no more exist as a national economy than does Bavaria or Alabama.

A Single European Currency would mean a federal superstate, like the United States but without its (not very good) national cohesion. Europe, politically divided by 12 languages, with populations which take little interest in each others affairs cannot even form a common public opinion never mind become a united democratic voice. Therefore all common action would be seen by the national electorates as illegitimate. Indeed this is precisely why "Europe" was created without asking its peoples.

No other region of the world is even proposing to unite their currencies (and therefore governments) — not even North America, and certainly not South East Asia. They are not so foolish. Indeed Asian countries point to the European Union as an example of what *not* to do and even the United States which has been instrumental (especially under the Kennedy, Bush and Clinton administrations) in helping to create the present European Union finds itself at odds with EU economic, exchange rate and trade policies and would not dream of involving itself in a similar constitutional State covering North America.

The Pound sterling is to British national democracy what a name is to an individual — without it neither can draw funds, spend or borrow as they wish, or even exist as a sovereign nation or as an independent individual. Many supporters of the abolition of the Pound (and therewith our sovereign nation) will claim that the abolition of all the currencies within the EU in favour of the Euro is no different from fixing currencies between nations. Needless to say, there is no comparison and the former link between the Irish punt and the Pound demonstrates why.

First, linking the Punt with the Pound in no way prevented movement of the Punt/Pound against other European currencies. Secondly despite the most intimate links which exist between any two European nations (investment, business, migration from Ireland to the UK, common language) the Irish were able to cut the currency link. Third it was when the Punt was able to find its proper level against the Pound that Irish assets and labour could be rationally priced by foreign investors in Ireland — so inward investment increased. This allowed many Irish people in England to return home and prosper where their hearts were — in their own homeland.

None of this has been possible within the EURO and as a result the Irish economy is out of control with 6% inflation but within the same currency as Germany with less than 1% inflation. The answer would be for Ireland to tax its own citizens or severely cut back on its Government expenditure but the Irish voter did not elect its government to do that. No government would dare to risk electoral unpopularity in order to appease the European Central Bank in Frankfurt.

When the newly emerged free nations of Eastern Europe escaped the Soviet communist yoke their first step was to create their own national currency. For with a national currency a nation "breathes" and shows that it really exists. A freely convertible currency (that was also Russia's first step after the break up of the Soviet Union) reflects real supply and demand, domestic assets, production value, overseas earnings and future prospects for all of these things.

Conversely when the Nazis marched into other countries in their plan to "integrate" the nations of Europe one of their first measures was to take over and control those nations' currencies. As a Rothschild once remarked, if you control a currency you control the nation. The Nazis had rigid controls of the currencies of the countries they took over. They set up a central bank in Berlin and organised a central clearing of payments — as a prelude to a single European currency. Real economic liberals and democrats know that you do not need a single currency to enjoy free trade. Dictators, fascists and the European Union know that you cannot control countries *without* abolishing their currencies.

A national currency also reflects the relative values of those who live in a country. (Some countries put more weight on leisure and families rather than production and wealth, some put religious observance before business interests, others reverse these priorities.) Climate and history also need to be (and are) reflected in the movements of national currencies.

3. NATIONS, REGIONS AND MIGRATION

A Single European Currency would mean that "regional economies" (at present represented by the nation states and their currencies which move up and down to reflect their specific economic conditions) would, like Ireland, be deprived of the natural and critical movement of their currency and would therefore have to find other mechanisms to restore economic balance. These would include:

a) massive inward social payments (from other regions- i.e. nations)

b) large outward migrations of labour (to other nations)

or

c) much higher taxes (imposed by the European Commission)

d) large inward migrations of labour (from other nations)

Either eventuality would mean burgeoning taxes and power flowing to the central "government" in Europe and mass migrations of labour across national/linguistic/cultural borders, heightening social alienation and political tension.

In America, where there is (only after the deaths of 600,000 in the civil war) one recognised government, one history and one language, over 7 million people move between states *every year*. Within the European Union this would be neither linguistically nor politically possible.

It is deeply ironic that, given the role of German and French political leaders in creating the European Union and driving towards further integration that the least crossed border in the European Union is that between France and Germany. (Their populations in their spontaneous choices totally reject the grandiose political schemes of their "leaders"). The stability of nations and their cultural cohesion depend on the retention of their populations and the stability of their families and opportunities for work. These in turn *depend on the flow of capital replacing the flow of workers*. This is the whole point of free markets in capital and it is all too typical of the real aims of the founders of the European Union that the alienation of migrating labour did not concern them.

But what has actually happened since the launch of the EURO, founded to give a cohesive single monetary market for investment flows? Has the one major economy, which has remained outside the EURO, suffered from a lack of inward investment? No — nor was this likely since there have always been large flows of inward investment into the UK dating from long before our membership of the European Union and inward investors need a free market in the currency of the nation in which they are investing in order to judge their (true) costs. The proof of the pudding is in the fact that since the UK decided to stay out of the EURO, foreign inward investment has reached record levels — £38.1 billion in 1998. Many of the investors are French and German companies escaping the enormous social and taxation burdens within the European Union! In the year to March 2000 inward investment rose 16% and since the Blair Government was elected in 1997 on a "wait and see" approach to the Euro *the stock* of inward investment has increased to £252 billion.

There is in fact a case for saying that there is too much inward investment in Britain since there are still vast subsidies available to foreign companies and those subsidies are providing an artificially high level of investment which in turn is boosting the level of the Pound to excessive levels against the Euro. If Government abolished the massive grants given to the rich shareholders of corporations like Ford or Nissan (the latter has received over £700million of grants for one factory in Sunderland alone) then:

1. British companies would not have to pay more tax to finance the subsidies to their foreign competitors.

2. There would not be the temptation to invest in the more risky ventures which are likely to end in failure.

3. The Pound would not be overvalued and therefore British exports would rise.

4. Foreign companies which have received such subsidies would not demand even more just to stay in Britain.

As in most crises from which Government claims it can rescue us, it was Government itself which brought the crisis about.

There are a number of important issues which could in theory give stability to an economy, even one the size of the European Union (assuming of course that it were possible politically). They are inward investment, convergence of different parts of the European economy and above all the movement of capital. If capital is free to move or is not inhibited by the burdens of regulation and taxation from moving *then it will flow to where jobs are in short supply thus making the migration of labour unnecessary.* But it is a sign of the true intentions of those who founded the European Union that it was the movement of people which interested them most, for that, rather than the free movement of capital would more quickly break up the cohesion of the nation states. (The cultural and linguistic alienation of those forced to migrate was of course of no concern.)

For such migration to be unnecessary large amounts of inward investment were necessary and it is the very country which has rejected the Euro, the United Kingdom, which has witnessed the greatest inflow of investment. There has always been large inward investment into the United Kingdom both because Britons have always been internationalist in their outlook and because of the large network of trading and financial operations based in the City of London.

If the Euro-zone countries provided a stable base for inward investors then that would increase job security and make migration of workers unnecessary but here again the facts show how those countries which have adopted the Euro are in fact breaking apart from each other. Far from converging they are diverging. The accounting firm Chantrey Vellacott found that the index of divergence of interest rates from their natural rate within each national economy of the Euro-zone worsened from 62 in January 1999 to 115 in October 1999 — zero would mean complete convergence. In other words (see Ireland above) an inward investor would have to reckon with great instability within the Euro-zone member states and therefore investment decisions become more difficult.

4. THE NATION'S CURRENCY AND THE NATION'S ASSETS

If Britain were to join the European Single Currency, we would contribute all our physical, financial and business assets to the EURO and to the State which that currency represents. Borrowings and liabilities in the European Union in general would be financed by international lenders looking to, for example, British oil, gas, coal (and pension funds) as *de facto* collateral.

The reason we never talk of "Scottish oil" but there is such a thing as "Norwegian oil" is because Scotland does not have its own currency (and is therefore not a sovereign nation) while Norway does. The Single European Currency would mean that in future North Sea Oil would be "European Oil". Indeed the European Treaties Britain has already signed refer to "common resources" which include of course physical assets onshore or offshore the UK. The European Parliament has on many occasions claimed that North Sea oil and gas are "European resources", not British and the entry of the UK into the EURO would finally bring that about.

While Britain would bring invaluable assets to the EURO, other member states bring massive liabilities, particularly in the form of unfunded future pensions. Germany's liabilities total 139% of annual Gross Domestic Product. France's liabilities total 98% of GDP and Italy's are 113% of GDP. This means that if the debt were spread across the European Union as a whole (and a single European currency of course does just that) it would cost the British people £1.2 thousand billion or £25,000 per head (source: House of Commons Social Security Committee).

The United Kingdom has the second biggest pension assets in the world after the United States. Britons can look to $2,000 trillion ($2,000,000,000,000,000) (source: *The Economist*) to secure their retirement — more than *all the other European Union* countries combined. Had we joined the EURO in January 1999 these pension assets would by now be worth $20 trillion less! Indeed it is odd that American corporations are still so supportive of the Euro, given that all their assets inside Euro zone countries are now worth at least 20% less than they were on January 1st 1999. They will have had to account for these exchange losses in their accounts. I wonder what their shareholders think of the great "European project" now?

5. FRAUD AND THE CENTRALISATION OF POWER

The Institute of Chartered Accountants has said: "The Euro will inevitably provide more opportunities for fraud. Money laundering across national frontiers is likely to become a major issue." There has already been a theft of sensitive printing materials used to print the Euro and the German banks have said that the security implications of distributing Euro notes and coins are so enormous that the German army will be needed to carry it out. We can only imagine what will be happening in Italy and the enticing prospects for the Mafia — although criminals are apparently quite looking forward to using Euro denominated large bank notes which are considerably lighter than lorry loads of Lira!

The Euro is being printed in most of the Euro-zone countries and in fact by British printing firms but it is not just the logistics of co-ordinating so many countries in one system of money printing and control but the extraordinary naive idea that so many different governments, central banks (which paradoxically carry on even in those countries which have abolished their currencies although it is not clear why) different taxation systems and different track records in even paying tax can run a currency when they have not even created one country.

But it is just such conflicts which are welcomed by the worst eurofanatics because they think that each crisis will lead to more central power, the consolidation of the new State and the destruction of the powers of the parliaments and governments of the nation states. One of Britain's leading economists Professor Patrick Minford was discussing the EURO with a member of the Bundesbank Board. The latter, when warned by Minford that the Euro-zone countries were courting a real crisis said that in fact they needed a crisis in order to consolidate the institutions of the European Union and the power of the European Central Bank. Such an attitude is not uncommon on the continent of Europe but would be unthinkable in Britain.

6. THE IMPLICATIONS FOR DEMOCRACY

If the United Kingdom should abolish the Pound then it will become effectively a local authority within the new country called "Europe". As any local authority in the United Kingdom knows they are ultimately controlled, have their budgets "capped" by and can be fined by central government. Even local councillors can be arrested (see the 1970s case of the Clay Cross councillors in Derbyshire). That is precisely the relationship between the real power in Europe (the European Commission and the European Court) and the "local" British Government. The Maastricht Treaty sets down the conditions under which the United Kingdom can be fined if it does not meet borrowing, spending and inflation targets set by the new Government in Brussels.

Gordon Brown, a proponent of the EURO, not long ago tried to bully the Bank of England to alter interest rates. If his EURO were to be imposed on Britain Mr Brown may as well retire — otherwise his bullying might land him in a (European) court case! Certainly, as Herr Lafontaine the German Finance Minister found out, there is no role for national control of money when a Government has abolished its currency.

Without complete political control by European institutions of *all* spending and borrowing within the countries which join the EURO, there will be fiscal and monetary chaos. *With* such controls there will be massive political rejection as voters within each "democratic nation" suddenly realise what has long been the case — that their national "governments" and "parliaments" are just puppets of a higher, unaccountable power. They will realise that virtually all their democratic rights and the powers of their parliament to represent them have been given away secretly behind their backs (without having ever been mentioned in any political party's manifesto) and that in fact their nationhood effectively no longer exists.

Indeed this is likely to become clear just when they are in the middle of an economic crisis. Such a crisis could come in Ireland where the economy is booming because the Euro ex-

78

change and interest rates are completely wrong for that economy or in Germany where there is still very high unemployment but also high interest rates (in order to counter boom conditions elsewhere and to protect the value of the Euro). This will lead to a downturn in economic activity and drive unemployment even higher.

In either country if the European Central Bank ordered the Irish or German governments to take action on government spending or taxation their respective electorates would say, "who are these unelected foreigners telling us what our government must do when we did not elect our own MPs on that platform?"

Of course such conflicts have already arisen on a daily basis in the political sphere where national parliaments and national courts are powerless to resist the arbitrary edicts of the European Commission and the European Court of Justice (sic). But it is in the economic sphere (where everyone understands what a currency is, for they have it in their pockets) that electoral resistance is likely to be strongest and where the resulting crisis is felt directly in job losses and higher taxes. This is why the final stage of the abolition of the free nations of Europe is presented as being "inevitable" — precisely because the euro-fanatics fear it is far from "inevitable" that the people will agree to it, or accept its consequences.

7. THE IMPLICATIONS FOR BRITISH POLITICAL PARTIES

It is inevitable that within a European Superstate of the kind which is nearing completion political parties would bear no resemblance to the British Labour, Liberal and Conservative parties which have arisen over centuries to reflect the concerns of a national electorate. Political Parties would represent not Conservatives, who believe in the nation state (since the nation state is being abolished) but Christian Democrats who believe in a predominantly Roman Catholic, Europe-wide superstate. They would not represent Socialism since the dominant left wing view on the continent is Social Democrat or Communist.

Needless to say a European union built on the abolition of nation states would not sporne Scottish and Welsh national parties or Ulster Unionist Parties.

The effects of EU membership on British political parties have already been considerable. The Labour Party is unable to intervene in the British national, regional or local economies (either to tax or to subsidise) without permission from "Europe". They could never impose import controls or protect certain industries; they could not take assets or companies into state ownership since this would involve infringing spending controls or subsidy/competition rules in Frankfurt and Brussels. Indeed when the Labour party tried to organise women only short-lists for the selection of Labour MPs they were forced by European Union law to stop the practice. Free market capitalists in the Conservative Party would be stuck with a EURO exchange rate which did not (and would never) reflect the true state of the British economy while Conservatives in general could no longer justify their party's existence since its very *raison d'etre* is the nation state.

British Trade Unionists would have no influence whatsoever since British unemployment would be of no significance to a central bank in Frankfurt which by law is concerned only with inflation nor would high unemployment in the "Euro-region" Britain be as important to the European Commission as the EU labour market as a whole.

Most social policy is already set in Brussels thanks to the Trade Unionists' support for the European Union's Health and Safety legislation and the Social Chapter of the Maastricht Treaty so British Trade Unionists will never again decide these matters and will be powerless if one day there is a majority within the EU to abolish such social rights — or indeed trade union rights in general! But that of course is the result of the loss of *constitutional* rights — sacrificed as we noted above in the blind pursuit of short-term *political* advantage.

One of the great and sudden converts to the abolition of the Pound in favour of the EURO in recent years is one John

Monks, President of the TUC, whose conversion came as a result of regular attendance at Bilderberg meetings during the early 1990s. As a result the leader of the TUC is a tireless campaigner for the EURO. Unfortunately its membership opposes the EURO by 61% to 15% according to an ICM poll. On 12th May 1999 a rally to promote the EURO failed - despite a stage-managed platform of 8 eurofanatics to one anti EURO speaker and a conference packed full of European Union propaganda. But since when has democracy ever had anything to do with the "European project"?

8. DOUGLAS HURD AND THE CONSTITUTIONAL DESTRUCTION OF BRITAIN

One of the chief architects of Britain's surrender of its national rights to self government was Douglas Hurd, the long time Foreign Secretary under the Thatcher and Major Tory Governments. It was he who bounced Mrs Thatcher into the Single European Act in 1986, selling it on the grounds that it was to promote "free trade" when of course it was one of the greatest of the many losses suffered by the British constitution since 1972.

Despite no mention in any Conservative election manifesto of the abolition of the currencies of the European Union and the possible abolition of the pound, Douglas Hurd signed the Maastricht Treaty on Economic and Monetary Union which said just that. Hurd later, having left office, said "I have never been an advocate of the Single European Currency ... it is a drastic proposal. ... every citizen in the high street in Europe will be told that what he or she has in his or purse will be trash." But it was he, by not using the British veto and signing the Maastricht Treaty, who had condemned every "every citizen in the High Street in Europe" to just that fate!

In a speech on 3rd February 1998, 9 months after the disastrous government of which he had been a leading member had departed, Hurd gave a speech to the CBI Northern Region members luncheon in which he compared the approaches of the Labour and Tory Parties to the Euro:

> One leader follows a policy of "wait, encourage and decide" the other "oppose, wait and decide". This is hardly a battleground of principle which is a relief to those of us who have never been enthusiastic about a single currency, but have accepted that British interests may induce us eventually to take part. Meanwhile British manufacturing and financial services have to equip themselves urgently to succeed in a world where the Euro is a leading currency, whether or not Britain takes part.

This short extract tells us so much about the weak, unprincipled waffle which has characterised the Establishment British politician since the 1960s and still grips the Tory party today. Naturally if you believe that the abolition of a nation's currency, central bank and Treasury is not a matter of either principle or constitutional concern then you are the kind of buffoon who will betray your democratic nation with the same lack of concern as you would choose a different suit. It is a "relief" to Hurd not to have to fight on a "battleground of principle" and he believes that under certain circumstances it can be in the national interest to abolish the nation! In this the equally "pragmatic" and constitutionally ignorant Blair of course supports him. Finally we get an insight into the economic illiteracy of the Foreign Office mandarin (for Hurd was more a civil servant than a democrat) when he predicts that the Euro will be one of the world's "leading currencies". The Euro continues to fail, even when the world economy has shown remarkably steady growth rates for nearly a decade and it is regarded with the same universal contempt as is the (ultimately treasonous) career of Douglas Hurd.

The author of this book had the opportunity to question Douglas Hurd after the signing of the Maastricht Treaty and just before its consideration by parliament in 1993. The then Prime Minister John Major had repeatedly claimed in public, in parliament and in interviews that the Treaty actually restored elements of British self-governance through the principle of so called "subsidiarity". I approached Hurd and said "Mr Hurd, you know that in fact the Maastricht Treaty, with its acceptance of the *acqis communautaire* and the continued recognition of the authority of the European Court of Justice means that not one iota of self governance will in fact be returned to the United Kingdom." Hurd replied "Yes, that is right." Was this a man who did not know what he was saying or was it someone who knew that his Prime Minister was telling lies?

On another occasion John Major, just before the second referendum in Denmark, said in Parliament that if Denmark voted NO then the United kingdom would not proceed with ratifying the Maastricht Treaty. A few weeks later, in the final week before voting Hurd visited Denmark and, asked whether Britain would indeed not proceed with the Maastricht Treaty if Danes said no, replied that that was not the case. This was of course a fatal blow to the Danish "No" Campaign.

It falls to few men in their lifetime to betray one country, but the Rt. Hon Douglas Hurd has achieved the unique feat of betraying two.

9. BRITAIN'S PATTERN OF INTERNATIONAL TRADE

Britain's trade and international investment patterns are totally different from *and irreconcilable* with most other EU member states. The percentage of the economy internationally traded and the international location of investment income differ greatly. British wealth in oil, gas and coal (traded in US Dollars) and the largest business investments in the United States economy mean that the important currency for British business is the US Dollar, not the EURO and yet we have never contemplated the surrender of our sovereign and democratic nation to the USA.

The remarkable characteristic of the British economy is its wealth of global, international investments. The total stock of inward investment by other countries in the UK in 2000 was £252 billion but the total stock of our investments overseas stood at £2,000 billion. After the USA Britain attracts more foreign inward investment than any other country in the world. In the year 2000/2001 (after two years of the *non-membership* of the EURO which eurofanatics claimed would be so disastrous) foreign direct investment in the UK stood at record levels. Investment projects rose from 757 the previous year to 869 and involved the creation of 71,488 jobs. Indeed this inward investment — has evidently been so spurred by non-membership of the EURO that it could now be regarded as a problem.

British exports to the European Union account for only 9% of Gross National Product. To allow the Union, through a Single European Currency to control our country and our economy for the sake of the 9% of our Gross National Product which goes to that small group of countries called The European Union is a madness of historical proportions — especially since that trade has for 25 years been massively loss-making. (Total deficit since 1972 over £150,000m).

European Countries *outside* the European Union trade far more of their GDP with the EU than does Britain. For instance Switzerland has always been outside the EU and yet 66% of its exports go to other European Union countries.

The EURO has, as this author predicted, already heightened trade tensions between Europe and the USA. While the international economy was slipping towards recession in 1999 and stock markets around the world had crashed following the economic crises in Russia and Japan, the European Union maintained its controls on imports of Russian steel and Japanese cars. The European Union, said the US Trade Representative Charlene Barschevsky, had left the USA to act "not only as the market of last resort but of first resort". The United Kingdom had equally been left in the lurch by our "partners" in the European Union when the Pound was collapsing inside the European Exchange Rate Mechanism in 1992, which ended in "Black Wednesday", the removal of a Chancellor of the Exchequer and the massive defeat of the Tory Party some years later. Those who claim to be our "partners" but who are in fact so totally out of kilter with the British economy and at best uninterested in or at worst antagonistic towards British interests will not, indeed cannot, change their policies to suit us. It is with the USA that we share language, trade patterns, legal systems, legal rights and vast mutual investments, not the countries of continental Europe.

Leading EU politicians always said that they wanted a "soft" EURO (that is a low exchange rate against other currencies) but even they could not have anticipated such a massive collapse of the currency against the Pound and the US Dollar — the latter by nearly 25%. This collapse has meant a large increase in Euro-zone exports to the USA and has made US exports more expensive in Europe. Prior to the advent of the Euro such "beggar thy neighbour" policies were not easy when 15 currencies needed to be co-ordinated. With one EURO, protectionist Europe has found in the collapse of its currency a weapon as potent as any tariff barrier — except that unlike illegal tariffs currency depreciation cannot be adjudged under world trade rules.

But it is not just against the Pound and the US Dollar that the Euro has fallen dramatically, it has also fallen considerably against the Japanese Yen since its launch in January 1999. Indeed Japanese funds which invested heavily in the Euro (believing German and French claim that it would be a "powerful world currency") were then forced to sell since under Japanese fund management it is obligatory to sell after assets have fallen by a given amount. Therefore for both the Japanese and American Governments, who have seen their Euro investments collapse, for Japanese and American investment funds and of course for Japanese and American corporations the dramatic fall of the Euro has wiped out billions of Dollars worth of assets. The collapse has of course also made Euro-zone exports to Japan and the USA artificially cheap, upset the whole balance of world trade and caused friction between the European Union, Japan and the USA. German Europe does not have to go to war in order to cause chaos in international relations.

10. THE EURO-DISASTER FOR GERMANY

Paradoxically it is the corporations of Germany and France which have done most to undermine the Euro by fleeing the Euro-zone for the USA and Britain. German industry has in recent years invested tens of billions of Pounds in the United Kingdom and hundreds of French companies have fled to southern Britain to escape the social, financial and employment consequences of the European Union and its falling currency. The total net outflow of investment from the Euro-zone since the launch of the Euro is in excess of £170 billion. If the proof of a pudding is in the eating then German and French companies are vomiting Euros.

Contrary to the lies of the "European Movement" the much-trumpeted Maastricht criteria for joining the EURO were never met. Only 3 of the 11 countries which "qualified" had met the debt levels set out in the Treaty by the time of the Euro launch in January 1999. Italy and Belgium had twice the levels of debt laid down in the Treaty. Neither Italy nor France had met the budget deficit limits but had "fudged" the figures by large one-off budgetary tricks. The Maastricht criteria covered government debt and spending levels and inflation but, crucially there was no Maastricht limit for unemployment which was (and despite recent falls still is) at crisis levels throughout the European Union. It indicates the grotesque lack of democratic accountability within the European Union and within the governments of France, Germany and Italy that very high unemployment was not a cause of concern to be included in the "convergence criteria" and that therefore the jobs of voters could be sacrificed on the altar of the budget and inflation criteria which *were* in the Maastricht Treaty.

The EURO, even before it was launched in 1999, had proved to be a very weak currency. Even in anticipation of the Euro the Deutschmark fell by about 30% against the Pound between 1992 and 1998 and has since fallen a further 12%, the most dramatic collapse of the German currency since the 1920s when the political and economic seeds of fascism and National

Socialism were sown. Had anyone sat down to deliberately re-create conditions of economic instability, social alienation and national resentment of 1930s Germany in the modern era, they could not have done better than establish the European Union and the Euro.

During his campaign to persuade his own countrymen of the wisdom of abolishing his nation's currency Chancellor Kohl was so worried about the rejection of the Euro that he asked the European Commission to stop "selling" the idea in Germany since it was making Germans angry and turning them against the abolition of the Deutschmark. It is a true fascist who forbids the truth in his own country — in case his people then reject his lies. But Germans — and Frenchmen — have always rejected the Euro, by between 60 and 90% in opinion polls (and continue to do so to this day after their national currencies have been abolished), but democratic accountability has never been a strong element in the authoritarian politics of continental Europe, as the arrogant characters of Kohl, Delors and Mitterand so often testified.

A former President of the German Central Bank (Bundesbank) said that a Single European Currency would mean a single "trade policy, finance and budget policy, social and wage policy ... in brief a federal state". The German people listened to their own economic experts and did not believe their "democratic leaders". There were two institutions in Germany which commanded the respect of the German people, both established in the post war constitution of 1949 — the Bundesbank and the Bundesverfassungsgericht (the Federal Constitutional Court). Helmut Kohl undermined both. The first was to guarantee the stability of the new Deutschmark so there could be no return to the wheelbarrow loads of confetti which the Reichsmark became in the early 1920s. One of the greatest Eurofanatic myths is that the German currency has proved more "stable" than the Pound. In January 1921 there were 64 Reichsmarks to the US Dollar. By November 1923 there were 4,200,000,000,000 Reichsmarks to the Dollar. Whereas the Pound has been in circulation for hundreds of years most continental currencies, like the long defunct Reichsmark, have been replaced in various "currency reforms" or simply disappeared as those countries' constitutions collapsed.

The Federal Constitutional Court was to guarantee the legal and human rights of the individual and the kind of stable and trustworthy constitutional democracy which Germany had never before experienced. The arbitrary suspension of the rule of law during the Weimar Republic and the enthusiastic adoption of those emergency laws by Hitler required a strong and publicly trusted institution which would lead Germans to trust their democratic representatives.

The very man who claimed to have re-established German unity — Helmut Kohl, destroyed the credibility of these two institutions. The first to lose its national credibility was the Bundesbank which Kohl forced to accept (following the fall of the Berlin Wall and the re-unification of West and East Germany in 1989) a ridiculous exchange rate at which "Ostmarks", the currency of East Germany, would be converted into Deutschmarks. Kohl was interested in buying as many votes as possible in the former East Germany to boost his chances of re-election. He therefore overruled the advice of the Bundesbank and fixed a conversion rate which gave an artificial boost to the savings of East Germans. Unfortunately that exchange rate also made East German industry even more uncompetitive than the previous communist regime had already made it! As a result there was a massive spending spree in East Germany and an equally massive exodus of East Germans to the West, where the infrastructure was scarcely able to absorb them. Naturally this grotesque behaviour by Kohl, interfering politically in one of the previously unpoliticised pillars of the German constitution, completely devalued the credibility of the Bundesbank and established a precedent for political manipulation of monetary matters, which was then applied with a vengeance to the abolition of the Deutschmark itself and the introduction of the collapsing Euro.

The Maastricht Treaty on Economic and Monetary Union which established the Euro was also the issue which led Kohl to undermine the other pillar of post war German democracy — the Federal Constitutional Court. The Court was called upon to determine whether the Maastricht treaty was compatible with the German constitution. It patently was not but Kohl's Government lied to the Court and put such pressure on it that one Professor of Jurisprudence said "Germany is no longer a law based state". In other words Kohl and his eurofanatic henchmen had effectively suspended the rule of law and substituted it with the rule of the arbitrary whim of politicians — the word fascism springs to mind to describe such antics, a fascist attitude so succinctly put by Kohl himself in his notorious statement that "might is right in politics and war".

Ironically it was Germany which was the first country to really suffer from the loss of its currency and therefore from the loss of self-government. The resignation of their Finance Minister, Oskar Lafontaine came after he had mistakenly believed that a) he was still finance minister of a self governing country, b) the Germany economy still existed and c) he could use his position as an elected politician to influence interest rates. Of course he eventually woke up to the fact that none of this was true — so, powerless as he was, he resigned. This extraordinary episode shows just how weak and vulnerable what we call "German democracy" has become in the new Europe, built ironically by German politicians.

Just as Douglas Hurd betrayed the democratic nation of the United Kingdom, so Helmut Kohl destroyed the prosperous democratic nation which was Germany. Was Kohl's recreation of all the characteristics of Weimar Germany and the power seeking, euro-integration policies of Hitler just accident and stupidity or was it intention and malice? Like all truly obnoxious movements in history it really does not matter. Whether by accident or intent politicians like Kohl, Major, Hurd, Cook, Blair and Mitterand seem to achieve almost identical outcomes to those desired by the more overtly evil. One of the greatest dangers in political history is to regard a few individuals who we *now* know did great evil as unique and whose death many years ago therefore removed the possibility of similar evils today. Hitler and Mussolini we *now* know did evil things but they were both originally socialist, they were both Roman Catholic, they were both leaders of parties which stood for election, they were both elected to power, they both had support among the British and European political elites. What better pedigree could a BBC interviewer wish? And yet ...

So let us look at just a few of the remarkable parallels in the life and work of Helmut Kohl and Adolf Hitler. Hitler in his school days used to rub out the borders of Germany in his Atlas. As a young man Kohl was arrested for ripping out border posts between Germany and France. Kohl said "might is right in politics and war", Hitler said "The world belongs to the man with guts — God helps him". Hitler said that Czechoslovakia had "got on the wrong train" and had no choice but to go the way Germany dictated "because the points were set that way" whereas Kohl claimed that "Germany is the locomotive of the European train" and if Britain was not careful it would "miss the train". Hitler destroyed Czechoslovakia and Yugoslavia and created petty nationalist states in Slovakia and Croatia. Helmut Kohl's German Europe has broken up Czechoslovakia and Yugoslavia, Slovakia driving out its gypsies, Croatia its Serbs and Albania its gypsies, Jews and Serbs.

Hitler established a personal election fund into which German and overseas corporations put substantial funds — Kohl faced prosecution for doing the same. Hitler's Nazis claimed that their integration of Europe was "fated" and "inevitable". Kohl said that "There is no alternative to combination unless we wish to challenge fate" and the constitutional treaties of Germany's European Union assert on virtually every page that it is "irrevocable and irreversible".

There are two great differences — whereas Hitler was confronted and defeated by Britain, the United States and their allies, Kohl recruited NATO on his side, (NATO even aiding the ethnic cleansing of Serbs from Croatia and Albania which Hitler and Mussolini had begun. Secondly whereas Hitler failed to integrate the free nations of Europe into an undemocratic German dominated superstate, Kohl succeeded.

Mass unemployment and deflation in Germany led the (socialist/green) Government to encourage trade unions to press for much higher wages with demands for 6 to 7% pay rises — where inflation is virtually zero. Since the German economy no longer exists this means that other countries within the EURO will have to pay for these pay rises — with higher unemployment or lower real wages or perhaps higher interest rates. (This is of course also true of the awards of subsidies and pay rises in France by the French government in attempts to appease striking farmers, fishermen, teachers and just about any group which has a grievance.) But, just like Oskar Lafontaine with the European Bank, so the Governments and electorates of those other countries have no power to influence German wage claims and settlements. The circle of irresponsibility and lack of accountability is very wide!

It has always been the cry of the economic illiterates who urged Britain into the European Exchange Rate Mechanism (ERM) and who support the permanent fixing of exchange rates in the EURO that everything would have been all right if "we had gone in earlier" or "at a different exchange rate". In fact of course there is never a good time to destroy currencies or fix prices. (How ironic that politicians who parrot the joys of a "dynamic economy" are the first to remove the dynamic movement of currencies!). Germany joined the EURO at an exchange rate which did not reflect its very high labour costs (40% more than in France, 50% more than in Italy or Britain and 80% more than in Spain. Really it now needs a big devaluation against the other EU countries in the EURO. *But it is now impossible since the Deutschmark does not exist.* Germany is therefore permanently trapped into a very high cost of production which will institutionalise its high unemployment — unless it can persuade other EU countries to pay themselves massively more, or persuade Germans to leave Germany in their millions to find work in other countries — but those alternatives would cause even more chaos.

In Germany as in the United Kingdom and other EU countries governments have acted without parliamentary approval, and where parliamentary approval was unavoidable they have acted without ever stating their intentions in a democratic manifesto. Where the overall aims of the Euro-State were set down in vague language elected politicians relinquished power to the European Court of Justice which daily makes laws by bypassing national parliaments and overturning without any democratic approval the laws passed by those parliaments. In the Council of Ministers, British and German ministers cast a vote in a forum in which they are outvoted and accept the majority *decision of other governments* about how their electorates should be governed *internally. Nothing could be more likely to alienate voters and destroy the delicate balance of democratic acceptability, which the Western allies had painstakingly built up in Europe in general and in Germany in particular, since the second world war.*

11. BRITISH BUSINESS AND THE POUND

One of the naive questions put to business about the EURO (requesting of course as usual a response "purely from a business point of view"!) was "Would the Euro provide currency stability for your business?" The naive businessman would then reply "Oh yes it would save me worrying about the change in the value of the Pound against the Deutschmark, Franc etc." But the whole purpose of currencies is to reflect the true size, nature and health of a national economy and its trade and financial relations with other countries. As with any other economic variable if it is fixed then it can no longer fulfil its function, the knowledge it imparts is no longer available and of course decision-making becomes more difficult. In addition when one variable is fixed other variables (like the balance of payments, employment or exports) must change more dramatically in order to re-establish a balance. Usually in times of poor trading conditions the Pound would fall so that imports could be curtailed, exports promoted and real wages fall in terms of other currencies, thus encouraging inward investment. But the abolition of the Pound would mean that taxes would have to rise to pay for extra social payments. (The unemployed are unlikely to move to other parts of the new single currency market since that would mean going to live (in large numbers) in other countries with all the linguistic, cultural and political alienation that would cause).

For businesses the putative saving on changing currencies would be more than balanced by a fall in profits, redundancy payments and a falling share price. *This is of course exactly what happened when Britain had a dress rehearsal for the EURO inside the Exchange Rate Mechanism.* Within 18 months unemployment had risen by 1.5 million, company bankruptcies had reached record levels, housing repossessions had affected one million people and billions of pounds were expended trying to support the unsupportable exchange rate to which the Exchange Rate Mechanism had committed us.

Such was the experience of fixing (and therefore effectively temporarily abolishing) the Pound between 1990 and 1992. But there had been a previous attempt by Chancellor Nigel Lawson in 1987 when he decided to "shadow the Deutschmark". On that occasion the "strong" Deutschmark fell in value and took the Pound with it, causing considerable inflation in the United Kingdom. In retrospect British "businessmen" (by which politicians usually mean the CBI!) on both occasions claimed that the idea was right but we "went in at the wrong rate". Needless to say this nonsensical excuse is now wearing rather thin. If two or more countries wish to abolish themselves then they should openly take the political decision so to do. The combining of parliaments, taxation and social policies might lead eventually to similar trade links, industrial policies, financial structures and social and political attitudes. If that point were ever reached those countries could perhaps abolish their separate currencies bit to put the currency horse before such a carriage is of course a recipe for disaster.

Those businessmen who wish to abolish the Pound because it is (at the time of writing, 2001) too high were not long ago saying we must join the EURO because the Pound was too weak (there could be no better example of why we should never make important political — never mind constitutional — decisions based on the "pragmatic" decisions of businessmen). In fact if the Pound is strong our earnings (although less in Pound terms) are much greater in terms of other countries' currencies — therefore we are richer. Indeed *all* our assets including the 80% of our economy which is not traded is also worth much more in world-wide terms.

If the Pound is weak then our exports become more competitive, and imports become more expensive. Therefore exports rise and imports fall. Thus a moving exchange rate restores balance without massive dislocation. The important thing about the Pound is that it reflects what is really happening *in our* economy, not in Germany's or France's or some fictional "Europe".

The bible of the businessman in Britain — and indeed internationally — is the London based *Financial Times* which in the modern era represents not so much the responsible owners of capital but the *collective ownership* of capital in the large corporations, pension funds and insurance companies which have so effectively mopped up the capital of those individuals, families and private businesses that used to flourish when the United Kingdom was a financial and entrepreneurial success. As the high point of corporatism the European Union has naturally been a great favourite of this corporatist newspaper which has been prepared to sacrifice the democratic constitution of the United Kingdom in the pursuit of the greater profits of its corporatist readers.

Not long ago *The Financial Times* gave support to the arch Europhile and former European Commissioner Sir Leon Brittan (a former Cabinet Minister sacked for misbehaviour and unelectable in the UK, who like that other electoral liability Neil Kinnock therefore made his lucrative career in Brussels where elections never take place). Brittan had asserted that the abolition of the nations of Europe will make war impossible. Of course if the nations have been conquered then there is certainly no need to wage war against them. And if they no longer exist then naturally they can no longer fight. But power does not just disappear and the abolition of sovereign competing nations means their replacement by a superpower without democratic credentials but with the kind of international swagger which is far more likely to cause wars than democratic nations going about their own business. A glance at the kind of arrogant supranational bullying characterised by the remarks of the great "integrators" of the European Union (see above chapter 2) will show the extent of that danger.

But the idea that if you abolish conflicting parties you abolish conflicts and that the larger a power becomes the more responsible, is the logic of tyranny throughout the ages and the logic of corporatism and collectivism during the 20th century. If competing companies are taken over by the state then you do not need to abolish competition. If the individual is merely a puppet of the State then we can be spared the conflict of free elections. If all personal capital is taxed away then we can abolish the conflicts inherent in competition. If all workers are forced into a closed shop then they cannot "conflict" with each other and big corporations can deal "efficiently" with only one monolithic trade union.

The disgraceful truth is that neither the abolition of the 11 national currencies (of the Euro-zone) nor the effective abolition of those nations' parliaments and the castration of their governments was ever mentioned in the manifesto of any "democratic" political party. The Euro and indeed the entire edifice of the European Union, designed from the beginning to abolish the free nations of Europe (in whose name the allies fought and won two world wars) were established by small cliques of corporatist, anti-democratic politicians and large multinational corporations behind the backs of voters, parliaments and democrats in every EU country. The house magazine of such multinationals is *The Financial Times* and when one of that paper's most successful journalists, C. Gordon Tether who founded the Lombard Column made no secret of his opposition to the European Union, the Bilderberg group and the corporatist threat to democratic nations, he was sacked. The Editor who sacked him was a certain Mr Fisher, a regular Bilderberg attendee. Fisher had removed sections of Tether's column which dealt with the Bilderberg Group and the Lockheed scandal of the 1970s (which involved bribery of politicians throughout Europe, including, in the Netherlands, the founder of Bilderberg, Prince Bernhard of the Netherlands). Gordon Tether's Lombard column was the longest running financial column in the world and the subsequent industrial tribunal in which he appealed against arbitrary dismissal became the longest in history — 18 months. (For a comprehensive analysis of the Bilderberg Group see *Europe's Full Circle*)

The Financial Times today reflects the views of the collectivists and corporatists who read it and who represent the new elite in our anti-democratic society. It is of course possible that, like our financial structures, the Financial Times will change again and reflect the values of entrepreneurial capitalism, individualism and democracy, but like the business interests they represent they are likely to be the last to be aware of and understand the winds of change.

As Benjamin Disraeli wisely remarked "The world is governed by very different personages from what is imagined by those who are not behind the scenes." It was precisely such "behind the scenes" manoeuvring by unelected corporatists which created the European union and its constitutional structures — under the mild sounding "Common Market". So successful have they been that they now think that the final step — the abolition of national currencies, national central banks, national Treasuries and (effectively therefore) national governments — is achievable.

Within the United Kingdom, businessmen who seek the abolition of the Pound are a small minority, but through the Confederation of British Industry (and their affiliated Chambers of

Commerce who pretend for propaganda purposes to be separate) they are accorded disproportionate airtime - especially by the BBC. Those thousands of businesses represented by the Institute of Directors (39,000 members) and the Federation of Small Businesses (125,000 members) are, like 75% of the British people, totally opposed to the abolition of the Pound and its replacement by the EURO.

The Confederation of British Industry was a strong supporter of the Pound's entry into the European Exchange Rate Mechanism — until it collapsed. Its predecessor, the Federation of British Industry (FBI) strongly supported the Gold Standard — the principal cause of the great depression. The FBI also supported Nazi industry, concluding major agreements as late as March 1939 in Dusseldorf. This was after Hitler's march into the Rhineland, the Nuremburg race laws, concentration camps, imprisonment of hundreds of thousands of political prisoners, the Kristallnacht attacks on the Jews and the invasion of Czechoslovakia). After the war senior FBI businessmen intervened with the Allied Administration of Germany to try to defend Nazi businessmen who had collaborated in the financial support of the Reich (including employing slave labour). The CBI has a unique track record and like all British businessmen who promote the Euro and the abolition of their own nation's currency, they cannot be trusted to grasp even the rudiments of democracy.

Foreign firms register their United Kingdom subsidiaries as members of the "Confederation of *British* Industry" — reminiscent of Michael Heseltine's fatuous statement that he was not interested in British companies but "companies in Britain"! Many of those firms — in particular Japanese companies — make frequent attacks on the Pound and propagandise for the EURO. Two such companies are Toyota and Nissan. Toyota has demanded that its suppliers invoice Toyota in Euros. This means that the suppliers, nearly all of which are smaller than Toyota, have each to change their Euros into Pounds. It is rational purely from a business point of view for Toyota, not its suppliers, to change pounds into Euros if they so wish since it is cheaper to convert the total amount than for each individual supplier to convert their shares. Therefore it is evident that Toyota is both passing on to its British suppliers the costs of its Euro losses and — particularly obnoxious in a democracy - making a public *political* point and thereby seeking to change policy within Britain. This is corporatism — the political involvement of collectives of capital and labour and their manipulation of democratic government.

But the supporters of the Eurostate know that big business, with its claims to speak for *all* business, in fact does nothing of the sort and it is therefore necessary to propagandise for support among the hundreds of thousands of small businesses. A report in the *Sunday Times* of 10th August 1999 was headlined "Small firms tout Euro as a stabilising force." The rising Pound had given the Euro-pushers a hope that British businessmen, their exports hit by the high rate of the Pound against EU currencies, would be duped into supporting a Single European Currency and the abolition of the pound as a solution to their problems. (As we noted elsewhere the corporatist and collectivist see the solutions to a crisis for "x" in the abolition of "x" rather than in tackling the original causes of the crisis.)

The article reported that the NatWest Bank was holding seminars "raising awareness" (!) of the Euro among small firms. In fact the writer had to admit that, according the Forum of Private Businesses, small businesses rejected the currency by more than two to one. Indeed 97% of the Federation of Small Businesses membership voted to leave the so-called "European Union" all together. Needless to say the NatWest Bank's devotion to "raising awareness" among Britain's small firms does not derive from a philanthropic desire to educate but rather from that organisation's own political agenda. The NatWest Bank is the driving force behind the "Association for Monetary Union in Europe" and their former Chairman heads the "Action Centre for Europe" which campaigns for the abolition of the Pound.

Small businesses, like the British people, are overwhelmingly opposed to the removal of these last vestiges of our democratic nation and our absorption into the German dominated Eurostate. But some banking and big business interests, supported by the European Commission, are desperately trying to seduce the naive in British business into surrendering their country for (supposed) profit. As we noted above in describing the "fourth technique" used by the euro-integrationists small businesses are asked not to worry their little heads about the loss of their country or parliamentary rights but are asked to decide "purely from a small business point of view".

Is it not strange that, after continental EU countries have collapsed because of their attempts to create a European currency, the NatWest Bank and its fellow corporatists suggest we could rescue ourselves (from our success!) by joining them in that very currency. Fortunately British small businesses are not so dim. Unlike their corporatist big brothers they cannot recruit the State to subsidise their failures so they are used to making decisions on commercial merit not on political grounds. (For those who wish to take action against those large corporations which like the Nat West Bank, have supported the worst elements of euro-fanaticism, see Appendix II.

12. BRITAIN OUTSIDE THE EUROPEAN UNION

One of the purposes of the European Union in general and the EURO in particular is to resist the "Anglo-Saxon" approach to liberal economics and politics. This has been made repeatedly clear by leading French, German and Belgian politicians. They say that the "Anglo-Saxon" system takes no account of the social costs of its policies and the State must therefore "control" business and economy to provide a more "compassionate" environment. But what do we see when we consider the results of this most "compassionate" approach on two apparently vulnerable sections of workers — women and the old? A recent study by the Centre for Policy Studies in London found that in France the real wages of the poorest female workers had increased by only 1% between 1984 and 1994 whereas in Britain the comparable figure (1985-1995) was 19%. In Germany the unemployment rate for older workers aged 55 to 64 was 14.5% in 1997 while in the USA it was a mere 2.9%. In Britain the unemployment rate in 1999 was 4.5% and the USA 4.5% while in Germany it was 11% and in France 11.4%. As we pragmatic Anglo-Saxons would say the proof of the pudding is in the eating!

London — and Britain — are at the centre of the world's finances and economy. Not only is the European economy far behind but in all except the field of financial derivatives (financial futures contracts) so is the USA. *London dominates the world in international banking, foreign exchange and foreign equity trading.* No wonder the European Union wants to get its hands on it — neatly packaged for them by the corrupt and ignorant British political classes. Their chief method of achieving this is the abolition of the Pound, the Bank of England and the take-over by the EURO and the European Central Bank in Frankfurt.

In 1999, despite the collapse of the Euro against the Pound (thus making British goods and services less competitive compared to Euro-zone countries like Germany, Italy and France) the United Kingdom was the 8th most competitive economy in the world (as well as being the 4th largest). By contrast those main pillars and drivers of the European union's "integration" agenda and members of the Euro — France, Germany and Italy were, respectively ranked 23rd, 25th and 35th in the world.

During the 1930s when large elements in all the three major political parties were appeasing Hitler and continental fascism, they tried to persuade Britons of the futility of resisting European "integration" (yes, the same words were used then) since the British Empire was of no value and the British economy could not possibly survive, never mind flourish in a world where nation states were increasingly irrelevant. They were tragically wrong then and they are even more tragically wrong now.

Today Britain is the fourth largest economy in the world, it is one of the five members of the Security Council of the United Nations (Germany for instance is not) one of the very few nuclear powers in the world, the biggest investor in the world's largest economy (the USA) a global investor with £2000 billion invested, the longest parliamentary tradition in the world, the longest surviving currency and the most stable currency in Europe. With the other nations which share our Anglo-Saxon heritage, language, parliamentary and legal traditions (the USA, Canada, Australia, New Zealand) we account for 40% of world trade (the European Union accounts for only 20%). So much for the predictions of the eurofanatics in the 1930s — and so much for their advice today.

13. BRITAIN INSIDE THE EUROPEAN UNION — TRAPPED IN THE SINGLE CURRENCY

The much vaunted "opt out" from the Social Chapter of the Maastricht Treaty was repeatedly shown to be worthless even before Tony Blair committed the United Kingdom "irrevocably and irreversibly" to its clutches by signing the Amsterdam Treaty in 1997. Close inspection of the Maastricht Treaty (not a common practice among the politicians who supported or signed it) reveals that even the opt out from the Single European Currency will prove totally impotent. The implications for the UK are so grave that no one who is serious about the constitutional imperative to save the Pound could accept the constitutional stranglehold of the European Union itself.

The abolition of the Pound, or, even if the UK rejects or postpones its abolition, continuing EU control of the British economy and currency, represents a grave and imminent crisis. Tragically this crisis — which could literally destroy what remains of our country — is in the hands of those who either believe in the abolition of the Pound, the Bank of England and the end of effective sovereign government in the United Kingdom or those who wrongly believe that if the UK refused to join the Single Currency we would be immune to the constraints of European economic and monetary union.

When considering the efficacy of the British parliament's controls over events in the European Union it is worth remembering that all Government ministers must (according to the Maastricht Treaty) have the power to go to any European Council meeting "authorised to take binding decisions for the Government of that member state". This is of course a grotesque denial of the very basis of democratic parliamentary governance — but then so is the entire creation and structure of the European Union.

In *The Times* of 3rd December 1996 it was reported that the then Chancellor of the Exchequer (Kenneth Clarke) had "won copper bottomed assurances" which answered the 'groundless fears' of the Conservative Eurosecptics". If the fears were groundless then why obtain copper-bottomed guarantees? But far more important was the naivety of a Chancellor claiming that (in the context of Treaties signed under European law and enforceable in the (political) European Court) "assurances" between politicians mean anything at all. For instance under Article 108, describing the controls exercisable by the European Central Bank over all Member States it specifically states that "recommendations and opinions shall have no binding force". In another context and in response to the specific requests of Heads of Government to open up EU discussions to public scrutiny, the European Court said, "their declarations were of an eminently political nature and therefore not binding on community institutions". So much then for Clarke's — or any other Minister's — "EU assurances"!

Unlike the Danish opt out from the Single Currency, which is quite clear, the wording of the UK's opt out is ambiguous and therefore dangerous. In addition Article 109k(2) seems to allow a majority vote of member states to force the UK to accept a Single Currency. The clause states:

> At least once every two years ... the Council shall, acting by a qualified majority on a proposal from the Commission decide which Member States with a derogation fulfil the

necessary conditions ... and abrogate the derogations (i.e. end the opt out) of Member States concerned.

In other words countries which do not want to change their opt out could be forced to abrogate such an opt out! The European Court of Justice which sees its aims as "promoting European integration" will resolve any ambiguity (although there seems to be none).

The constraints of the Single Market alone are certainly sufficient to let the European Court of Justice impose economic and exchange rate controls on the United Kingdom even if we are outside the Single Currency. (see below.) Any appeal to the Council of Ministers to overrule such a judgement would have to contend with the kind of attitude expressed by for example a former French Prime Minister Alain Juppe and a former Belgian Finance Minister who rejected competitive freedom for those member states currencies which are outside the EURO. As many of us pointed out to British Ministers in the mid 1980s when the ludicrous "Single European Act" was signed, the provisions had nothing to do with competitive economic markets but everything to do with single political control. Needless to say the freedom to pursue "beggar thy neighbour" policies by those *inside* the Euro does not seem to be affected. The Euro-zone economies, without enforcement of the Single Market rules (and the EU majority which decides whether to apply them is *within* the Euro), thus enjoy a massive and artificial competitive advantage against the Pound. Like so much else within the European Union it is not the law which rules but the politicised majority which decides whether the law should be applied.

Article 109.1. of the Maastricht Treaty allows for the European Central Bank (albeit with a possible UK veto which in the hands of a Gordon Brown could not be relied upon or in the hands of a government trading off other interests might not materialise) to "conclude formal agreements on an exchange rate system for the EURO in relation to non Community currencies". In other words not only will Community countries which do not join the Single Currency be coerced but also political power will be used to "negotiate" fixed rates with *any* country in the world. This is economic fascism in its true imperialist mode.

Article 108a(2) of the Treaty of Maastricht makes clear that the European Central Bank shall issue regulations "binding in its entirety and directly applicable in all member states" (NB *not* restricted to those states which join the Single Currency). These regulations can be applied to "the prudential supervision of credit institutions and other financial institutions". (ECB Statute 25.2)

The Maastricht Treaty protocol which describes Britain's "opt out" from stages 2 and 3 of monetary union is chaotically drafted. On the one hand it says that "unless the UK notifies the Council that it intends to move to the third stage of monetary union it shall be under no obligation to do so": on the other hand it states "Paragraphs 3-9 (the opt out clauses) shall have effect if the UK notifies the Council that it does not intend to move to the third stage." So we cannot tell from the wording whether the UK needs to actively opt out or passively just fail to opt in. This means yet more opportunities for the arbitrating European Court to adjudicate in the true spirit of the political integration which it admits is its overriding aim.

Whether the UK opts out of abolishing the Pound or not the Bank of England must subscribe to the capital of the European Central Bank and transfer "foreign reserve assets and contribute to reserves on the same basis as the national central bank of a member state whose derogation has been abrogated" (i.e. which has joined the single currency) (UK opt out clause 10b). Furthermore the amount of European Central Bank capital demanded of EU member states can be increased by majority vote. In other words the UK would have to contribute more capital to something it had opted out of!

Whether the UK opts out or not Article 9.1 of the protocol on the European Central Bank will apply. (must be read in conjunction with Article 8. of Protocol on UK opt out). This allows the Bank to "have legal personality (and) enjoy in each of the Member States the most extensive legal capacity accorded to legal persons under its law; it may, in particular, acquire or dispose of movable and immovable property and may be party to legal proceedings". And all this they could do in the UK even if we had permanently opted out of a Single Currency!

The former Chancellor of the Exchequer Kenneth Clarke used to claim that the Government had no intention of re-joining the ERM and yet he wished to retain his option to join a single currency. But it is impossible to join the Single Currency without having remained "within the normal fluctuating margins provided for by the Exchange Rate Mechanism of the European Monetary System without severe tensions for at least two years". (Protocol on convergence criteria Article 3). It is precisely this level of ignorance among leading politicians of all parties, which has permitted the effective destruction of the British constitution and which now threatens to hasten the end of the last crutch of our nation's sovereignty — the Pound Sterling.

There is an array of other duties even for those member states which have opted out of the Single Currency. For instance Article 102a states:

> Member states shall conduct their economic policies with a view to contributing to the achievement of the objectives of the Community (note NOT the objectives of individual member states)

> Member States shall regard their economic policies as a matter of common concern and shall co-ordinate them within the Council (of Ministers)

In a European Commission paper on Stage 3 of Economic and Monetary Union, there is no mention of "opt outs". Only two categories are mentioned "ins" and "pre-ins" — not surprising, given the general approach described above. The status of the "pre-ins" would "be merely transitional". A new ERM is proposed for those member states *not* in the Single Currency which makes the former Conservative Chancellor's belief in the avoidance of the ERM even if the UK chose to enter EMU even more extraordinary.

Throughout the tragic relationship between the United Kingdom and the European Union, the British people have been plagued by the failure of their "democratic representatives" to even read the Treaties they were signing on our behalf. As a result Ministers' daily impotence in the face of the onrushing juggernaut of the new Eurostate seems to surprise them.

There is in fact but one remaining crutch for that sovereign nation for which 1.2 million people died in two world wars — the Pound Sterling. The actions of the last Conservative government fatally undermined even that last proud bastion of our democratic self-governance. The utterances of the Labour Chancellor and Prime Minister, who seem totally unaware of the constitutional, political and even fiscal implications of the Single European Currency, can only be described as surreal.

There is one clear way of avoiding the difficulties and traps for the United Kingdom set out here — to take advantage of the illegality of the entire enterprise of European Economic and Monetary Union which Norris McWhirter and I described in our book *Treason at Maastricht*. (The Germans never ratified the Treaty as signed and therefore the treaty, under any normal democratic rule of law, would fall. The fact that the juggernaut carries on regardless is itself proof of the inherently fascist nature of the enterprise.)

Indeed even remaining within the "European" Union while others press ahead with a single currency has already gravely threatened the stability of the British economy — although not by as much as membership of that currency would have entailed. The catastrophic dislocation of labour and capital markets which a failed Euro will cause will require enormous social and regional "cohesion" spending to bridge the fissures caused by imposing a single monetary regime on so many disparate national and regional economies.

Such expenditure will require a large increase in community funds which can only be agreed by unanimity of member states. Since the consequences for the British fiscal purse (and every other member state's finances) would be grave it is extremely unlikely that a principal paymaster — like Germany or the UK — would vote for such additional funds; equally those countries which at present benefit from massive subsidies for agriculture (like Ireland) would almost certainly veto any loss of subsidy to those regions which had lost industrial jobs as a result of EMU.

Unable to react to massive unemployment in certain regions and countries, unemployment would rise and national budgets would breach the strict financial terms of the "Stability Pact". In addition the innate protectionist forces of Italy, France and Germany would undoubtedly react against a tragedy of their own making by restricting the exports of "perfidious Albion". The political costs within the EU are already being felt in the rise of extremism in Germany and France and the external view of the Euro has already led to widespread selling on international markets and the migration of capital to the UK, the USA and other parts of the world. (Recent estimates are that $170 billion has been exported from the Euro-zone since the currency's foundation.)

The French and Belgian politicians quoted above assumed that those currencies which stayed outside the EURO would be weak while the EURO would be strong. As a result they threatened to apply trade controls on imports from those countries which stayed within the European Union but did not join the "strong" Euro! In fact of course (as one has come to expect of the predictions of Euro-leaders) the exact opposite process has resulted, with those countries likely to join the EURO being weak. Needless to say there is no talk of protecting British industry against the predatory priced imports from e.g. Germany, France and Italy whose currencies collapsed even in *anticipation* of their membership of EMU.

So long as the United Kingdom "went along" with European integration in order to prevent it, there was logic behind our vetoes. As soon as we refused to use those vetoes, the catastrophe on the continent was inevitable and we should have long since withdrawn from the political "union" to that relationship which the British people approved (but did not obtain) in 1975 — that of a free trading group of sovereign nations, without budgetary or political commitment.

This (inevitable) move will require the kind of *volte face* which will frustrate a large section of the British and continental political Establishments but it will be less devastating than the electoral holocaust when the people eventually awaken to the loss of their nations and democracies.

As the former head of the American Federal Reserve Board, Lawrence Lindsey, noted "I am somewhat unsettled by the secretive nature of the federalist agenda. I am not sure that when European electorates discover they have surrendered national political sovereignty by adopting a single currency they will be altogether pleased." Surely the understatement of the century!

CHAPTER 4

GERMAN EUROPE COMES FULL CIRCLE

1. A EUROPEAN HISTORY LESSON — CHARLEMAGNE

Charlemagne, or Karl, as he is known to Germans, was crowned in Rome in the year 800 as the "Holy Roman Emperor of the German Nation", thus combining in one person and one concept that hegemony which arises when the political mission of the Vatican and German Imperialism find common cause on the continent of Europe. From the bloody bigotry of the Frankish Charlemagne to the massacres by Catholics of Orthodox Christian Slavs in the 20th century, history has shown how dangerous such a common cause has proved to be for the peoples of Europe. For those who believe that "time has moved on" we need only to witness the secretive machinations of Joseph Retinger who saw himself as an agent of the Vatican when he founded the European Movement, the Catholic imperialism of the Pan European Movement in the 1930s and today and the following words by the leader of that movement, Otto von Habsburg:

> Now we do possess a European symbol that belongs to all nations equally. This is the Crown of the Holy Roman Empire which embodies the tradition of Charlemagne the ruler of a united occident. It should therefore be considered whether the European head of State as the protector of European law and justice should not also become the guardian of the symbol which more than any other represents the sovereignty of the European Community.

Of course Charlemagne never ruled a united occident even 1200 years ago and certainly not today, but those who seek to build a new European empire must not only destroy nations and the history and allegiances of those nations, they must establish a set of myths and allegiances to replace them. All this of course is precisely what von Habsburg, whose family lost its throne and its empire, now seeks to create as a replacement fiefdom!

During the 1999 elections to the European Parliament the organisation which spent vast sums of money praising the wonders of the European Commission and the European Union was called "The Charlemagne Group of Companies". It was based at "Charlemagne House" in Hove, Sussex. The Charlemagne Prize, awarded by the City of Aachen (Aix La Chapelle), the historical capital of Charlemagne's Europe, was awarded in 1999 to Tony Blair, the British Prime Minister.

I suppose it is possible that Tony Blair had no idea who Charlemagne was and what he did and therefore what significance he has for those on the continent whose aim it is to destroy the self governing nations of Europe. Equally the vast majority of English Catholics have little or no knowledge of the imperial-political programme of the Vatican and indeed oppose the kind of politicised religion which promotes "the European project". Certainly this author, while warning of the dangers of the Vatican's politics has much sympathy with Catholic moral teaching. The danger arises where an absolutist faith is used to promote supranational political goals.

Blair, despite being brought up in an Anglican (Chorister School, Durham) is married to a Catholic, his children attend Roman Catholic schools and he attends mass in a London Roman Catholic Church. This all undoubtedly helped the City of Aachen to award him the prize named after the 'Holy Roman Emperor' Charlemagne.

After a German radio station's listeners complained that a prize devoted to the 'peaceful integration of Europe' could be awarded to someone who had killed over 2,000 Serb civilians (including 60 Albanian Kosovans) and had deliberately bombed and killed journalists in a Serb television station, a spokesman for the Charlemagne prize told the London *Evening Standard* "the prize does not refer to peace in the strictest sense of the word"!

The reason why this prize to promote European integration is not called the Hitler Prize or the Napoleon Prize is firstly because people can remember the evil deeds of these two 'European leaders' and secondly because their attempts to 'unite Europe' failed. Charlemagne on the other hand was crowned Holy Roman Emperor long before the printing press and long enough ago for even historians never mind voters to remember his deeds. Charlemagne did succeed — for a while — in creating a European superstate. But how did he achieve it?

While Christianity flourished in Britain and Ireland in the 8th and 9th centuries, paganism, following the defeat of the Roman Empire, began to re-assert itself in central Europe. East of the Rhine was predominantly pagan where ancestor worship and sacrifice were accepted as the natural order.

It was the English Christian, Boniface, from Crediton in Devon, who set forth to Christianise the German tribes and unlike the merciless, murdering, empire building Charlemagne, he used only his bible and his persuasive powers as a man of God. He was murdered in what is now Holland and his bible which is today in the Cathedral city of Fulda, ostensibly bears the mark of the sword blow which killed him.

Charlemagne was from the 'Christianity by the sword' school of diplomacy and born of a Frankish warrior aristocracy, which had been Christian since the 6th century. Having deposed his brother in 771AD 'Charles the Great' (whose throne is still in Aachen and gives historical resonance to the 'honour' bestowed on Tony Blair) started his campaign of bloody conquest of Saxony, Bavaria and Lombardy. In 782AD 4,500 prisoners were murdered by Charlemagne's army in Northern Germany.

Charlemagne, like the modern Roman Catholic Church, took monotheistic Christianity at its word and slaughtered those who refused to believe in their God or indeed believed in no God. Charlemagne's edicts included:

"If anyone follows pagan rights, let him pay with his life."

"If there is anyone of the Saxon people unbaptised let him die."

"If anyone is unfaithful to our Lord let him suffer the penalty of death."

Not surprisingly the 'European' Union's prize for those who have done most to destroy the nations of Europe is called the Charlemagne Prize. Long after Charlemagne had created his empire at the centre of western Europe and been crowned Holy Roman Emperor in 800, he was still confronted by the mighty Godefrid, King of the Northmen who built the massive Danework from the Baltic to the North Sea. Before meeting on the battlefield the Danish leader was murdered whereupon his son concluded a peace treaty with Charlemagne. (An interesting modern day equivalent was the second Danish referendum on Maastricht — the Danish people having got the answer wrong in the first referendum!). With the anti-democratic weight of corporatist capital behind the free spending government this murderous attack on Danish democracy resulted in a 'yes' vote. As we noted (above Chapter 3 part 8) our own government and our Foreign Secretary, Douglas Hurd, played an ignominious role. As far as I am aware there was no *British* equivalent of Douglas Hurd to betray the Danes in Charlemagne's time!

Charlemagne's bloody conquest of most of central and western Europe having been achieved in the name of Christianity, he was advised by the eminent English theologians — in particular Alquin — that killing people was not a very good way of converting them. Inspired by the intellectual liberalism of Bede and the theological centres of Jarrow and Lindisfarne, Charlemagne officially renounced violence in 789 and he turned to education through monastic teaching. (The European Union, now that the democratic constitutions of the nations have been destroyed has taken to propagandising in British Schools and Universities). Charlemagne's monasteries became centres of religion, general education and publishing. He then looked to Rome for approval and was subsequently crowned Holy Roman Emperor in AD 800. (After his exertions in the name of Charlemagne's modern European Empire, Helmut Kohl, a week after his electoral defeat, made a visit to the Vatican).

This latter, educational phase of Charlemagne's empire building cannot of course erase the evil of his original murderous conquests. Nor can such politicised 'education' (so akin to that practised today by the European Union) be regarded as a harmless activity. That today, among the new Charlemagnes of the 'integrating' European Union, such a man can be revered — and that a British Prime Minister could be honoured to receive a 'Charlemagne Prize' is extraordinary. But it adds historical and religious weight to the mountain of political, economic and constitutional evidence against the 'new Europe'.

2. DESTROYING THE FREE NATIONS OF EUROPE — HOW THE TRAP WAS SET

To their amazement and utter joy the German political class realised that others in Europe saw the peaceful solution to the problem of Germany in a blueprint virtually identical to that which German imperialism and fascism had wanted in the first place.

Their task was made easier by a well planned long term process which, step by step over many years, led the political and corporate classes of the once free nations of Europe to agree voluntarily to the end of their rights as democracies and sovereign nations.

In German there is a turn of phrase which recurs often in political discourse — *"Die Weichen sind gestellt"* (the points are set). Another railway metaphor often used in the process of bullying the nations into surrender to the Euro-State is "the train is leaving the station" and those who do not accept a European Superstate by hastening to the next stage of surrender will be "left behind". Another metaphor used by, among others, Helmut Kohl to suggest inevitable movement was the idea of the "convoy". Kohl said, in exasperation when he could not bludgeon all the members of the European Union into accepting his Superstate under German control, ludicrously said that "We cannot wait for the slowest ship in the convoy" — thus of course completely contradicting the whole purpose of a convoy which is to stick together.

But the German phrase "the points are set" is the most interesting and the most arrogant assumption about the "inevitable" destruction of the democratic nations of Europe. It suggests that the course of events which the speaker wishes has been set some way back down the track and it is therefore right and inevitable that we must travel the pre-ordained journey. This is part of the German idea of political "destiny" or "fate" which are also words frequently used by Kohl — and his predecessors in the Third Reich. Hitler used the "points are set" threat against Czechoslovakia just before he invaded.

In a democratic society of course the idea that anything (apart from the democratic constitution itself) is inevitable is in itself a contradiction of democracy. But the German corporatist classes and continental fascism in general have always sought *to make* what they wanted inevitable. This was done by a deliberate "setting of points" at a very early stage which would produce very specific effects, structures and institutions "further down the line" — i.e. decades later.

First of all there was the post 1945 decision to establish a "Coal and Steel community" with France — an exact replica of the strategy pursued by Germany after the First World War. Then came the innocuous sounding (but not at all innocuous constitutional structures) of the Treaty of Rome in 1956. *Like so many other schemes of the euro-federalists the intention was not so much to succeed and thereby bring prosperity to the people but to fail and thereby bring extra powers to European wide institutions.*

There was an excellent chance — especially given the nature of authoritarian, *dirigiste* continental politics — that the rules of free trade within the "common market" would be disobeyed and that therefore a stronger central legal power would be required to enforce those rules. Hence there arose a central legal system and a central court to make law on its own account and not be constrained by mere treaties — nor by the democratic parliaments of those nations which had signed those treaties!

Continental *dirigiste* governments which make much of their rejection of "Anglo-Saxon free trade" naturally so distort capital markets that there have to be severe adjustments in other economic areas — like unemployment and labour migration. This naturally requires an ideal excuse to break down the borders between nations, which in turn requires a new "trans-national" passport (a contradiction in terms) and then the assumption of a pseudo "citizenship" to define those within the new borders. These borders — unlike the national borders based on history, language and tradition — are of course purely arbitrary, based solely on the exclusion of neighbouring states because they do not suit the internal structures, prejudices and aims of the European Union.

Having thus so distorted industrial markets and national allegiance there is born the idea of the "Single Market" which supplants national markets. A "single market" is of course a contradiction in terms since free trade (which the word "market" seems to denote) is a general principle which does not restrict itself to a particular geographic or political entity. But the real idea behind the "Single Market" *was not a free and fair market but a stepping stone to a single State*. The eurofederalists knew that the single market constructed for big business and the new empire of bureaucrats in Brussels would demand "harmonised" terms of work, a "harmonised" social security system and a "harmonised" tax and pensions system.

Having therefore introduced, "purely for business purposes", a central system of economic and social controls the role of the nation state could then be portrayed as "getting in the way" of the "rational" and "pragmatic" conduct of business. The final step in the elimination of the nation state was the single currency, the Euro. In turn it was constructed "logically" on the single market — thus revealing of course the true meaning of that term. The forcing of incompatible economies, political systems and governments into one currency would produce enormous tensions. The different countries would have widely different levels of inflation, interest rate requirements, balance of payments positions and spending and taxation requirements but one currency would be applied to all. The need for action to serve the new State would not be recognised by its constituent parts so they would not act in its service. The problems would get worse until, in order to "restore order" the new central state bureaucracy would impose its will. Out of this chaos would come not a fully fledged central bank with "authority" but a single taxation system and a single "national" treasury. Knowing the implications of the Euro for events "further down the track" as it were the German economics minister said at the launch of the EURO:

> The EU needs economic policy co-ordination — national policies would jeopardise the process.

Out of such logic the dominant power is bound to be the country with the biggest population and the biggest economy with the most central position — Germany. Once these relationships of centralisation and dominance have been established in the business and economic sphere the exact same logic is applied to foreign and defence policy. It was Hans Eichel, the German Finance Minister who said recently:

> Why do the 15 EU states still need 15 foreign ministries and 15 diplomatic services? Europe would be stronger if it spoke to the outside world with a single voice. Why do we still need individual national armies? In Europe one army is enough.

And how is such dominance in the fields of defence and foreign policy achieved? — in the same way as in the economic sphere, by causing and managing a crisis. That crisis was

116

Yugoslavia where throughout the 1980s the German intelligence services, operating in conjunction with Croat nationalists (often those closest to the former fascist regime in the wartime puppet state of Croatia who had fled to Germany after the war) undermined the state of Yugoslavia. The head of the German Intelligence Services in the 1980s was Klaus Kinkel, later to become Foreign Minister. The Germans armed the Croats and Albanian terrorists and (following the Vatican's recognition) recognised the state of Croatia on 23rd December 1991. The new Croatia then established an extreme nationalist constitution and expelled 40,000 Serbs. The way to war was clear and the German political class had its "crisis" for which it could call on ignorant American and British politicians (Clinton and Blair, Albright and Cook) to use NATO's might to support our historical fascist enemies (Croats, Bosnians and Albanians) against our historical anti-fascist friends — the Serbs.

The disgraceful demands of the Rambouillet Accord could never be accepted by any nation state and the concocted stories about Serb "concentration camps" and the blaming of Serbs for the Sarajevo market bombing (later the UN admitted it was Bosnian Muslims who were responsible) were the excuses for war against what remained of Yugoslavia.

So this continuing crisis gave Eichel and the German political class the excuse to demand more defence and foreign policy co-ordination and to demand a single army. The greatest irony was that it further gave German Europe the opportunity to pose — after the fall of Milosevic — as the "rescuer" of Yugoslavia and the supplier of funds to rebuild what its own crusade had destroyed.

Two further pillars of the new German Eurostate have been constructed by the "setting of points" in response to supposed crises — often crises caused by the very European Union institutions which now claim to be able to resolve them — the extradition of citizens and the establishment of a European Union wide judicial system. The excuse for both was crime — but the kind of supranational crime which the European Union itself, by its own activities, greatly encouraged. The grotesque and corrupt Common Agricultural Policy (with large claims for subsidies for non existent crops, the smuggling of animals across borders, the large payments for intervention stocks to maintain prices and the fraudulent claims for export subsidies) and the Common Fisheries Policy (with its attempts to control fishing while subsidising fishermen and applying quotas to certain kinds of fish in certain areas) all these fundamental structures of the European Union provided a multitude of opportunities for supranational European fraud — and therefore even greater opportunities for Eurofederalists to establish a supranational European wide system of law which would override national jurisdiction. The infamous *corpus juris* can be imposed on the nation states of the European Union without any veto because it claims to tackle fraud. So yet again it is a crisis of the European Union's own making which leads to the extension of its power.

The European Extradition Conventions do of course cover more countries than those in the European Union but the creation of an assumed "European citizenship", with "freedom of movement of persons" across borders and the loss of border controls on goods traffic (and agricultural produce) all created heaven-sent opportunities for the criminal — and thus an even more welcome excuse for the creation of cross border law and a further decimation of the rights of democratic nations to enact and police their own laws.

The North American Free Trade Agreement (NAFTA), unlike the various European Union Treaties, has always been an agreement between sovereign nations for the promotion of cooperation and free trade (much as the European Common Market was sold to the people of Europe!) and therefore there was never any prospect of a supranational agency taking from or giving to US citizens any individual or collective rights. The European Union however from the very beginning included in its embryo constitution (i.e. the treaties) the assumption that the higher authority of European institutions could overrule national parliaments. As a result individuals within each and every member state can be extradited automatically to another state — in the same way as the Third Reich arranged in the 1940s. According to the terms of the 1940 Franco German Armistice Agreement (Article 19):

> The French Government is bound to surrender on demand all German subjects designated by the Government of the Reich who are in France or in the French possessions ...

Today, according to European Conventions on Extradition and (for the UK) the 1989 Extradition Act all "European citizens" may at any time, without presentation in court of any *prima facie* evidence, be arrested and taken to Germany for trial. *But Germany has exempted itself from extraditing Germans on the same basis.*

Indeed there are several other examples of Germany exempting itself from the treaties it has forced on others in the name of European integration. International law allows abducted children of divorced or separated parents to return to the country where they had previously lived but Germany repeatedly refuses to do this. There are many cases of child abduction (illegal in most countries) effectively condoned by the German State — if the abductor is a German!

Germany is of course the signatory to a number of human rights conventions and yet it has blatantly discriminated in cases where a patient living in Germany is refused an organ transplant if they cannot speak German. Indeed *a law was specifically passed* giving the German Doctor's Council the right to refuse treatment in such cases. German speakers, a doctor claimed, "have a better chance of success"!

These examples of German national or even racial discrimination and many other political and economic assertions of their national will contradict their whole propaganda which describes the European Union as putting an end to "narrow nationalism". But the reality is as usual far from the rhetoric. German nationalism and its historic "destiny" have created a straightjacket for others and a platform for domination for Germany — all in the name of the "European Union".

Germany's increasing domination of Europe is based not so much on destroying nations in general but only *those which have proved to be stable non-racial nations and bastions against German ambitions* — like the UK, Switzerland, Czechoslovakia and Yugoslavia. For if Germany can isolate nations on the grounds of race then by definition Germany becomes the most powerful racial nation. By constructing an empire called "Europe" it places itself at the centre of that empire. By selling the Euro as an aid to trade, it establishes the central bank for that imperial currency in Frankfurt. With the help of those free nations which defeated its 20th century ambitions, the German political and diplomatic class has returned to Berlin where it has a superb view over its "lost territories" and an eastern barrier to its ambitions, Russia, lies in ruins. By using the European Union to spread its commercial and industrial tentacles across the continent and even into those countries which have not yet joined the European Union (Hungary, Poland and Czechoslovakia) it begins to assert its political agenda with "common" European foreign and defence policies. By pushing (as far as the British Foreign Office is concerned) at an open door of EU expansion towards the East Germany fulfils its historical ambitions so eloquently summed up in the phrase *"Der Drang nach Osten"*.

Finally let us look at the words of those who have constructed this German Europe.

"Might is right in politics and war." —Helmut Kohl, German Chancellor

Many Jews survive today "thanks to the circumstance that they were forced Labourers and not directly killed by the SS. Germans are tired of philosemitic over-compensation in the media and sterile grief Rituals by politicians." — Professor Lutz Niethammer, Historical Adviser to the German Chancellor Schroeder (2000).

"The Jews should consider whether they would have behaved heroically if they had not been victims of the persecution." — Klaus von Dohnanyi, Former Mayor of Hamburg (1998).

German Intelligence Service under Klaus Kinkel (Foreign Minister under Kohl) from 1981 starts (with over 100 agents) to infiltrate and undermine Yugoslavia. — E. Schmidt-Eenboom, German Espionage Expert in *Der Schattenkrieger*, EconVerlag, Dusseldorf, 1997.

All "European citizens" may at any time, without presentation in court of any prima facie evidence be arrested and taken to Germany for trial. But Germany has exempted itself from extraditing Germans on the same basis. European Conventions on Extradition and (for the UK) 1989 Extradition Act.

And all this has happened with the full co-operation of those nations — Britain and the United States — which have abandoned free enterprise democracy in favour of that very collectivism and corporatism which characterises continental fascism. German Europe could not have wished for a more decadent "West" and a more ignorant and dangerous political class than that which ruled in London and Washington DC throughout the 1990s.

3. THE FASCIST NATURE OF THE EUROPEAN UNION

The new European Union, despite its growing power, is still manipulating and bypassing democratic systems and creating oppressive anti-individual, anti-democratic structures. For instance a report written for the European Commission which showed that high unemployment coincided with high taxes and social regulations in industry was deliberately not published. So much for democratic openness.

An internal memo of the European Commission said *"the Commission should not get carried away by the idea of transparency — it is necessary to learn to conceal aspects of information which give rise to bad interpretation."*

Not long ago before the European Summit in Amsterdam, 27 Danes were put under 'preventative arrest' in case they made trouble at a European Summit — by that they mean demonstrating outside the summit. We have already seen above the massive interventions of the European Commission in the schools, universities and television programmes of the nations they seek to destroy.

That is "the country called Europe" today. Now the European leaders of this "New World Order" are increasingly bold in the assertion of their new powers and their new empire:

"The European Union would require a European Army to fight the resource wars of the 21st Century." — Jacques Delors:

"German troops will be engaged for the maintenance of the free market and access without hindrance to the raw materials of the entire world." — The German General Naumann, also a NATO Commander.

"As applicant members of the European Union they are required to join in our regulations." — A German spokesman on the pressure on Serbia's neighbours to join trade embargoes (an act of war) against Serbia during the Kosovo war.

So that is the world into which Edward Heath, John Major, Sir Geoffrey Howe and Douglas Hurd have plunged us, with the grateful cheering of Labour and Liberal Parties in the United Kingdom. It is an evil world planned secretly and constructed undemocratically behind the backs of Europe's electorates. The pernicious censorship of the truth by the newspapers and in particular radio and television even in Britain, historically seen as the bastion of democratic nationhood, is unparalleled. Even more incredible is the collaboration in this venture of the United States which fought two bloody wars and engaged in a detailed denazification process at the "heart of Europe" after 1945. The Americans must soon realise that the democratic nations of Europe for which so much blood was spilt has all but disappeared. Europe has gone full circle.

4. ADOLF BLAIR AND THE FASCIST NATURE OF MODERN BRITAIN

In Tony Blair's election address at Sedgefield in 1983 the politician who now wishes to abolish the Pound, the Bank of England and H M Treasury in favour of the EURO and the Frankfurt central Bank, this future prime minister and putative "leader" of an integrated Europe, asserted:

> We will negotiate a withdrawal from the EEC which has drained our national resources and destroyed jobs.

In his first full year in office Blair voted in only 14 of the 325 divisions of the House of Commons and since he entered Downing Street he has introduced new election systems for Britain's European Parliament elections, for the Northern Ireland assembly, for the Welsh Assembly, for the Scottish Parliament and for the London Mayor and London Assembly. Each of these elections is held on a different electoral system, depending on which result Mr Blair and his cronies desired. (In the case of the abolition of the House of Lords Blair replaced appointment by God (birth into the nobility) with appointment by Blair — and his successors.) Arbitrary rules decided by the rulers to suit themselves is a classic definition of fascism.

Just before the 2001 general election there was a sudden resignation by the MP for St Helens South, a Labour seat with an overwhelming majority. Because the MP made his announcement after the election had been called the Labour Party's emergency rules came into force which meant that Labour Headquarters was able to impose a short list of candidates on the local party. A Tory defector to Labour, Shaun Woodward (formerly member for Whitney and a former BBC producer) was manipulated into the seat.

While preparing for a referendum on the latest "settlement" in Northern Ireland the Labour Government, in a leaked internal Northern Ireland Office memorandum said "We have commissioned research without it being seen to be government inspired. It is important to ensure that not all results of opinion polls be in the public domain as some will be important to our cause and others will not."

Small farmers in Britain are committing suicide at an alarming rate, some 400 over the last three years compared to a figure of 27 deaths from vCJD. A document issued by Gwent Police called on all their employees, whether police or just general staff to act as spies on farmers. The appeal was for any information on "farmers meetings or congregations", demonstrations, "any conversations overheard, suspected movement of farm vehicles and any information from unusual sources i.e. internet or CB radio". Here in Blair's Britain were ordinary British citizens being called upon to act as spies for the state against desperate but law abiding fellow citizens.

The true extent to which fascism has entered Blair's Britain through the machinations of the European Union can be seen in the attempts by europhiles within the British political Establishments to create, without electoral consultation or democratic approval, regional governments within England. Scotland and Wales were never logical "regions" but their recognition as regions by the European Commission was a political act designed to create the petty nationalistic states which would destroy the United Kingdom as effectively as that principle has broken up Czechoslovakia and Yugoslavia.

In recent years the British Labour Government (consciously or unconsciously it matters not) has done the work of the euro-federalists by giving more and more power and responsibility to "Regional Development Agencies" — which are *also* nationally based in Wales and Scotland! Recently the Government has organised regional "constitutional conventions" to which the major political parties, trade unionists, "business leaders", representatives of the European Union and even the churches have been invited. In all the regions where this agenda has been pushed hard there is a remarkable symmetry between those promoting these conventions and the members of the European Union's "Committee of the Regions" and other EU front organisations. We can also note the essentially corporatist nature of these gatherings — i.e. only those who belong to a group or collective are invited to form the organising and committee structure. This was always the characteristic of fascist systems. The individual voter is excluded or only allowed to express an opinion when the entire system the corporatist wanted is a *fait accompli.*

I set out in Appendix III the extraordinary report of the proceedings at one of these "conventions" which demonstrate without doubt the fascist nature not only of this European Union inspired regionalism but the sinister change in the political life of Britain after the Major-Clarke-Kennedy-Blair axis replaced British democracy with European corporatism.

It is therefore more than appropriate to examine the character of the man who has managed to create in one of the oldest parliamentary systems in the world, which twice fought the tyranny of German imperialism and European fascism, a society which is unrecognisable as British, tolerant, democratic or free. Political beliefs and more particularly political actions are all too often the public expression of private psychoses and this is particularly true of Tony Blair, whom this writer encountered as a schoolboy in Durham when Blair, although only aged 8, displayed his extraordinary meddlesome, arrogant character by telling pupils, monitors and teachers how the school should be run! This did not make him popular and the inevitable repercussions by his elders and betters bred the kind of resentment which at best coloured but more probably determined his political development.

The most cogent and convincing explanation of this individual is to compare him with those who had a similar personal development, a similar ideological development and party career, resulting in a devotion to a European integrated "superpower" and an ambition so manic and ruthless that the party, colleagues, democracy and even nationhood which had moulded him became expendable. In this there is one obvious comparator — Adolf Hitler (1889-1945) (and for certain characteristics his ideological admirers and sidekicks Oswald Mosley (1896-1980) and Benito Mussolini (1883-1945)).

Mussolini, like Hitler and Blair, began his career in a socialist party. Like Blair he sought to create a cult of personality around himself and a cult of modernism infused his politics. As with Blair his desire to remove the power of traditionalists and those of superior achievement and intellect led him to embrace the notion of modernism as a means of expunging the historical achievements of the "forces of Conservatism". Both Blair and Mussolini, once they had used traditionalist socialists to achieve power sought to project the power of their "new society" overseas — Mussolini in Africa and Blair in the Middle East and the Balkans.

Within the United Kingdom it is perhaps with Mosley that Blair can best be compared, for like him Mosley was a British socialist, indeed a Labour cabinet minister who courted both big corporations and "the common people". Mosley left the Labour Party and founded the "New Party" much as Blair has effectively created a new party in "New Labour". Both Blair and Mosley were sure of one thing; they could not be Conservatives for they were creating a "new" party for a "modern" world in the "new" Europe. Both of course sought to ally themselves with the power of Germany but neither were really comfortable friends of the essentially selfish and nationalistic German State elite. Both flirted with the worst forms of Irish nationalism, Mosley, rather more overtly than Blair, proposing the "re-unification" of Ireland.

But it is with the twice constitutionally elected leader of the National Socialist German Workers Party, Adolf Hitler, that builder and putative leader of a united, integrated Europe, with whom Blair has, personally, psychologically and politically the most in common. I set out below a table of comparison between Hitler and Blair which must be taken as a whole. Any *one* element in the character of either could of course be shared by any number of politicians who would not or have not represented a grave danger to their electorates. But I submit that the number of such comparisons are deeply disturbing and explain much of what has happened and could happen to the United Kingdom.

TONY BLAIR	ADOLF HITLER
Father an orphan.	Father illegitimate.
Father a Conservative.	Father a Conservative.
Split between Scottishness (Father) and Britishness (his personal power base).	Conflict between Austrian origins and Germany (his power base).
School activist, meddlesome. Exaggerated stories of his youthful adventures (flying alone abroad as a schoolboy!). Unpopular at school but good at disguising the fact from those who matter (Headmaster thought he was popular).	Hyperactive — disappointed when other pupils would not carry on playing cowboys and indians! Unpopular at school but figure of authority, like Hitler's Jewish doctor Dr Erhard Bloch said "What a nice pleasant youth Hitler was."
Resentful of authority.	Resentful of authority, resentful of Conservative background and schooling.
Joined Socialist Party then abandonned "Clause Four" Nationalisation	Joined German Labour Party, then pushed through abandonment of nationalisation of industry.
"New Labour" — combined flag waving pseudo nationalism with pseudo socialism — "Blairite Party".	Nazi (National Socialist German Workers Party) referred to as "the Hitler Party".

Used party to get power then marginalised party and concentrated on apparatus of State power.	Used NSDAP to get power then ignored party and ran a State apparatus under the "Fuhrerprinzip" — leadership principle.
Contempt for Parliament — worst voting record in Commons. Committed troops to Yugoslav war by Royal Prerogative. Parliament admitted its illegality.	Enabling Act (March 1933) gave Hitler powers to rule by non-parliamentary order.
Used attack on Yugoslavia to boost profile at home and among EU leaders.	Used military adventures (1935 March into Rhineland, attack on Czechoslovakia etc) to boost popularity.
Democratically unapproved steps towards integration, the Euro etc. Corporate greed will do much of his political work for him (eg Euro).	Ruled by decree.
Courted big business, received big donations for Labour Party from multi-nationals, recruited senior executives of BP, Northern Foods, Sainsbury's, Barclays into government.	Big multinationals like BMW, Ford, General Electric contributed to Hitler's personal election fund.
Used political statements by Ford and General Motors to promote EURO.	Hitler awarded Henry Ford highest civilian order in 1938. General Motors described by the US Ambassador in Berlin as "a war danger" for their aid to German industry.

Award of peerage to owner of the *Daily Telegraph* — followed by very favourable coverage, especially during 2001 election campaign	Nazis gradually intimidated and took over opposition press.
Constant urge to re-construct — e.g. school systems, health systems, the constitution of the UK, the House of Lords and 5 different electoral systems (depending on the result Blair wanted)	Hitler saw himself as designer, an architect. He needed to re-design and rebuild cities. Saw his architectural sketches as his "most valuable possessions".
Sees himself as a man of destiny (reference in speech before 1997 election to "a thousand years")	Hitler and the Nazis frequently referred to their "destiny" and the "fate" of Europe and the "Thousand Year Reich"
So convinced of his fundamentally just and compassionate destiny that the end of nation, parliament, democracy in creating "superpower" and people power. It is in the national interest to abolish the nation.	Hitler's glory was not in the nation but in the Reich (German European Empire). Nation, Parliament, democracy gave way to the Reich, the State, the "People" ("People's Court", the "People's Car" etc)
Constant appeal to greater convenience and profits for business. Urges big business to prosper from an integrated Europe	Hitler (like the Kaiser) used the State to promote big business. Great opportunities in the new Reich. Business (e.g. I G Farben) financed State intelligence activities abroad.
Used "humanitarian aid" excuse to attack Yugoslavia	Used "humanitarian aid" excuse to invade

(declared illegal at Nuremberg trials).	Czechoslovakia.
Refuses to appear to answer war crime charges at International Court.	Never put on trial. Suicide.

It is difficult to apply the words national socialist and fascist to politicians without seemingly accusing them of inherent evil. But that is not my intention. I am not saying that either Hitler or Blair were inherently evil, they merely pursued grand ideas based on socialism, corporatist capital, an integrated European superpower and a managerial elite working independently of the party which brought them to power. The kind of crushing manipulative state which they both created served the "big players" with "big ideas" needing "big structures". (If this sounds like a recent grotesque Barclays Bank television advertisement then Barclays is of course one of the main supporters of the European Union and the abolition of the pound!)

And the result of this psychological and political common ground is clear not only at the constitutional level but in the kind of tyrannies Blair's Government supports, comparable in every way with the evils of the Nazi period. While ethnically cleansing 500,000 Serbs from Croatia and killing civilians in Kosovo and Belgrade Blair has diplomatic relations with religious bigots and extreme nationalists in Israel which has an official policy of assassinating political opponents. While refusing to appear before the International Court to answer war crimes charges Blair has diplomatic relations with the fascist and racist regime in Zimbabwe. While pursuing what his Foreign Secretary called an "ethical foreign policy" Blair welcomes Irish nationalist murderers into government in Northern Ireland alongside those they tried to murder. Sinn Fein/IRA are of course extreme nationalists and socialists (ie Nazis) — just like the German Nazis they tried to aid by planting bombs in London during the war.

Neither Hitler nor Blair were evil. But the former did evil and the latter has adopted an astonishingly large number of the former's ideas, the most significant of which is to absorb the once sovereign democracy of the United Kingdom into the new German Europe. It is perhaps only when the historically ignorant Blair realises that he will not after all lead this new empire that he may remove his dangerous rose-tinted spectacles and see this ill-defined "Europe" for what it really is. For "Europe" is the embodiment of the historical ambitions of German imperialism and continental fascism, whose principal aim has been to counter and defeat that very system of Anglo-Saxon liberal trade and parliamentary democracy based on the common law which Blair claims to love.

5.   DER DRANG NACH OSTEN — GERMAN THREATS TO POLAND AND CZECHOSLOVAKIA

The following is a translation of a motion put down by the then governing Parties — Christian Democrats and Free Democrats — and passed by the German parliament on 7th July 1998. The motion was "Refugees, evacuees and German minorities are a bridge between the Germans and their Eastern Neighbours". My translation, in bold italic, is followed by my comments. The motion reads as follows:

"The expansion of the European Union to the east represents for Germany and for the whole of Europe a great opportunity."

Note which comes first — Germany, which shows the use of 'Europe' not as a means of suppressing German nationalism but as a means of promoting German national interests.

"Democracy and the Rule of law in middle and Eastern Europe will be lastingly secured through the entry of our neighbours into the European Union and the Atlantic alliance. Step by step we are thus approaching (My em-

131

phasis) the common goal of a lasting and just peace for the whole of Europe."

Most Europeans had assumed this was achieved in 1945 after the defeat of the Nazis — or at least in 1989 after the defeat of communism but not so apparently for a still agitating German political class.

"The Germans who were expelled from their homelands, the expellees resident in Germany, as well as the German minorities in middle and eastern Europe have supported from the beginning the policy of opening up the countries of middle and eastern Europe and have been actively involved in the development of this process. Today we see how the Charter of the German Expellees of 5th August 1950 has become reality. In this charter the expellees, a few years after war, flight and expulsion declared their support for a Europe 'in which the peoples can live without fear'."

This is precisely why the Poles, Czechs and others who had suffered from both the Kaiser and the Nazis' aggression, persecution and murder, drove out the German minorities, who had collaborated in that persecution, in the first place.

"The German parliament calls on the Federal Government to actively pursue its consistent policy in support of German refugees, late evacuees and German minorities in the East and to continue effectively to represent their justified concerns.

1. The German Parliament supports a policy of a comprehensive inclusion of the German refugees, evacuees and German minorities in middle and Eastern Europe in Germany's co-operation (sic!) with its eastern neighbours. The German Parliament welcomes the inclusion of the representatives of the Sudeten Germans in the institutions (!) established by the German-Czech declaration of 21st January 1997."

A typical example of how the promise of EU and NATO membership has been exploited by German Europe to 'persuade' the Czechs to 'co-operate' with the (now exiled) Sudeten Germans who welcomed the Nazi invasion of 1938 and helped the Nazis to persecute the Czechs.

"The participation of suitable representatives of the Sudeten Germans on the board of the German-Czech 'Fund for the Future' and in the co-ordinating council of the German-Czech forum are an important contribution to reconciliation and mutual understanding as well as for a fruitful dialogue between Germans and Czechs."

This is all so reminiscent of the German 'friendship organisations' set up in the 1930s with those countries which were later invaded and subjugated.

2. *"Even during the political upheavals in East and South East Europe, but especially after the fall of the wall and barbed wire the German refugees sought contacts in their original homelands and provided much support* (Constant reference to their 'homelands' infers a continuing claim, indeed even a nationalist claim.) *The German Parliament reasserts its unanimous resolution of 28th February 1997 on the 'Contribution of the German refugees to the reconstruction in Germany and to Peace in Europe.'*

Even today the integration of Europe is already making easier the promotion of German culture in the homelands of the refugees. (In other words in Poland, Czechoslovakia etc. as the Poles, Czechs and others know to their cost!) The German Parliament welcomes the fact that more and more state and private institutions in middle and eastern Europe, especially in the fields of science, art and culture are concerned with the continuing German cultural and historical inheritance in those areas and are co-operating with cultural and scientific institutions in Germany, especially those of the refugees. Parliament expects that the Federal Gov-

ernment, the states and local councils will promote this process in the future."

How precisely this mirrors the experiences of Norway before the Nazi invasion. As Churchill described in *The History of the Second World War* "for some years past Nordic meetings had been arranged in Germany to which large numbers of Norwegians had been invited. German lecturers, actors, singers and men of science had visited Norway in the promotion of common culture ... The President of the Norwegian Parliament has written: 'The Germans under the mask of friendship tried to extinguish the nation ...' what stupefied the Norwegians was that men and women who had been cordially welcomed in one's home were spies and agents of destruction." The European Union has now extinguished the self-governing nations of Western Europe and the German political class now wishes to do the same for Eastern Europe.

3. *"The German Parliament, in accordance with the treaty agreements with the states of middle and eastern Europe and most recently with the ratification of the German-Polish and German-Czech 'Neighbour treaties' has emphasised that in the process of the acceptance of our eastern neighbours into the EU and NATO, basic European freedoms must of course be equally applied without condition to all citizens in the old and new member states, including the German refugees."*

Note once again how NATO, as in the latest war in the Balkans, is seen by Germany as the (credible) power behind which German Europe expands. Treaties between neighbours are not usually necessary unless there is tension, grounds for mutual aggression or territorial claims. This kind of treaty, coupled with the European Union treaties, now shows precisely what Germany intends with its promotion of 'Europe'.

The creation of one 'Europe' with it's 'citizens' who have 'equal rights' throughout its territory and then the expansion of 'Europe' eastwards permits the re-colonisation by Germans of those countries whose suffering under German rule led to the expulsion of German minorities in the first place. Even if these areas of e.g. Poland and Czechoslovakia were today populated by Germans (never mind when they are not) the aggressive promotion of cross border cultural and financial institutions would represent a political and territorial threat to those countries.

Helmut Kohl's claim that only by creating a united Europe would German aggression and war be prevented was the exact opposite of the truth. For it is precisely through those 'European' institutions that the mechanisms for expanding German influence and control, especially towards the East, have been constructed. This is only 'peaceful' in the sense that it makes aggression unnecessary!

> *"The German Parliament expresses the hope that with the entry of the Czech Republic and Poland into the European Union the acceptance of common ownership (!) by the new member states will permit the solution of unresolved (!) bilateral problems. That would include the right to free movement and freedom of settlement (!)."*

Here we have expressed in ruthlessly clear words the true purpose of the EU's economic (the 'single market', freedom of movement) and its political characteristics (freedom of residence of 'European citizens', non-discrimination etc.). What can be sold to the dimmer British politician as free trade and free investment becomes a political tool for the re-colonisation of eastern Europe and a threat to all the small nations within which Germans once lived ('Freedom of settlement' and even 'common ownership'). What can be sold in western Europe as a fight against racism and xenophobia can be used in the east to prevent Polish and Czech resistance to German migration and cultural imperialism.

> *"They are important elements in the realisation of the goal of a united Europe, in that peoples and ethnic groups with their different cultures and traditions can live together in harmony while having regard for their historical common-*

ality and mutual respect and promotion of their different identity ... They are the elements which are intended to help overcome the consequences of war and expulsion."

In other words to overcome the settlement of the last war, whereby Germans were driven out of those countries in which they had proved aggressors against the native majority and had helped the Nazi state to conquer those countries. (There never was any 'historical commonality' or 'mutual respect'.) This is not quite what Western Europe had in mind by a 'united Europe'. Nor would such politicians agree that the 'consequences of the war' should be reversed! In all these calls for the peaceful co-existence of minorities in a united Euro-state we must be aware of how, historically and during the 1980s and 1990s, Germany undermined and destroyed the multi-ethnic state of Yugoslavia, recognised Slovenia, its Wartime fascist puppet Croatia then rearmed and helped the 'Kosovo Liberation Army' in its attempt to wrest a part of Serbia from Serbian control and finally sending troops and planes for 'peacekeeping' bombing runs in a war which they had instigated.

"Expulsion must not be regarded as a legitimate means to achieving political ends."

This is precisely what Germany supported when Serbs were driven out of their historical homeland in the Krajina by the Croats (having been declared an alien minority by the Croatian constitution). 'Expulsion' is also the result of the war in Kosovo where Serbs have again been ethnically cleansed from their own country (from 50% of the population after the 1st World war to less than 5% today with much of that cleansing presided over by United Nations forces).

Is it not strange that, just as in the 1940s, it is Germany's hated Slav enemy (Russians and Serbs) who suffer while former Nazi allies (Slovenia, Slovakia, Croatia) flourish?

4. "The German Parliament therefore shares the approach of the Federal Government — and indeed all other post war governments — which has always seen the post war expulsion of Germans from their historical homelands as a great injustice and illegal. The parliament calls on the Government to continue its dialogue with the governments of our eastern neighbours and stand up for the interests of the expellees."

Now we see in more aggressive language what all the friendship, co-operation, cultural exchange and 'united Europe' really adds up to. It is apparently perfectly legal for Serbs to be driven out of their own country but not for Germans out of other people's countries.

5. *"The position of minorities is of decisive importance for a lasting peace* (*Friedensordnung* — literally peace order) *in Europe. Such minorities can form an important bridge between European states and peoples. The minorities and ethnic groups in Europe can perform their bridging function more effectively the more their cultural, linguistic, religious and ethnic identities are respected and protected."*

This is the ultimate hypocrisy from a government, which defines its own citizens according to blood and does not permit it's 'guest workers' from other countries to vote in Germany. It is the present and historical attitude of the German state to its 'blood brothers' in other countries and its promotion of their right not to integrate into the linguistic and cultural life of the countries in which they live that permanently destabilises other nations. This 'bridging function' seems to apply only to Germans in other countries where they no longer live but into which 'European citizenship' will entitle them to return at the cost of the indigenous peoples. The Italian government does not take such a position about Italians in England, nor does the British government about Englishmen in France or in the USA — so why does Germany?

"The German parliament welcomes the framework agreement of the Council of Europe of 1st January 1995 on the protection of national minorities which was ratified by the German parliament in 1997 and became law on 1st Fe-

137

bruary 1998. The German Parliament expresses the hope that our eastern neighbours, for example Poland, Latvia and Lithuania will ratify this document as soon as possible (Those countries are rightly hesitant to sign agreements which their historical enemy embraces with such speed!) *Like the European Charter for Regional and Minority Languages of the Council of Europe of 5th November 1992, which is at present in the process of ratification in Germany, this framework convention contributes to the improvement of the legal position of the German ethnic groups and minorities in middle and eastern Europe as regards their legal status and political representation and the maintenance of their culture and language. In this convention the German parliament calls on the German government to actively pursue their policy of support for German minorities in middle and Eastern Europe."*

Once again we see how 'European' charters and treaties have been carefully worded to promote exclusively German interests in Eastern Europe.

6. *"... The German Parliament welcomes the offer of out-of-school German courses in the CIS (former Soviet Union) by the German Government. It calls on the Government to continue and expand these initiatives..."*

One wonders how this promotion of the German language inside other countries is appreciated by the indigenous peoples. There is a difference between language courses for ethnic Germans who wish to return to Germany on the one hand and for those who do not on the other. The latter will certainly not be encouraged to integrate into their 'homelands' by learning German for the first time. But the extent to which only blood is the deciding factor for German citizenship is clear when the German language qualification has to be taught artificially!

7. *"The German Parliament supports the common task of anchoring throughout Europe the culture of living together which has developed through European integration ... A Europe which is drawing together with the*

138

*inclusion of states in middle and eastern Europe cre-
ates the preconditions for a common formation of the
European future."*

Many small countries in Europe — west as well as east —
have fought two wars in order not to have their 'common' future decided by others and certainly not by a European superpower of the kind which the German political class has been
creating since the end of the last war. National sovereignty and
the co-operation of free nations in trade, social relations and
frequent political alliances is precisely what that war was
fought to achieve. In 'middle and eastern Europe', as this German parliamentary motion calls it, we see the difference between that concept of free nationhood and the coercion of other
nations dressed up as 'co-operation', and 'cultural exchanges'
and 'European integration'. Europe has indeed gone 'full
circle'. Ironically and tragically this has happened with the full
collaboration of the British political establishments.

6. GERMANY AND THE BREAK UP OF CZECHOSLOVAKIA

On the 27th and 28th February 1992 (during the final negotiations of the Maastricht Treaty on European Economic and
Monetary Union) German Chancellor Helmut Kohl travelled
first to Prague and then to Bratislava on the occasion of the
signing of the German-Czechoslovakian "Treaty on Neighbourliness and friendly Cooperation". The Kohl visit was reported
in full in the German *Archiv der Gegenwart* for 1992 and it is
from that report that I quote below.

The Kohl visit showed all too clearly how Germany encouraged Slovakia (its war time ally) to break away from Czechoslovakia, pointing out how the new "Europe" would be built on
"regional" lines and that therefore Slovakia, with German help,
would not need to be part of Czechoslovakia. It also shows
how, even in the 1990s — and today — the tensions over the
1938 take-over of the Sudetenland by Nazi Germany cannot be
reconciled and no satisfactory wording could be agreed in that

139

regard for this new "Treaty on Neighbourliness and Friendly Cooperation". The Kohl visit also showed how the old German diplomatic tricks of "regionalism", "joint projects" "cultural ties" and "border co-operation" (not to mention the fundamental weapon of "European citizenship") are deployed to achieve the political, economic and demographic re-occupation of Eastern Europe.

I will start by looking at the final part of Kohl's visit, when he met Prime Minister Jan Carnogursky and the president of the Slovak National assembly Frantisek Miklosko. In his meeting with Carnogursky:

> ... the most important topic of the discussions was the federal construction of Europe.

The report goes on to say that Germany was already very active in Slovakia. Many German companies had already concluded agreements to establish joint ventures with Slovakian companies. Kohl went on to speak with Miklosko where:

> the German Chancellor emphasised at a press conference the desire of the German Government to accept its eastern neighbours into the European Union. The great opportunity for Slovakia lay in a Europe of Regions.

Needless to say Germany had no right to offer acceptance of Slovakia into the EU since such a step would be a collective decision of the 15 members of the Union, but such a use of the EU by German diplomats and politicians either to entice or threaten other nations now has a long track record. Equally such ideas and such methods were also used in the 1930s as Germany set out to "integrate Europe".

At the beginning of the report the *Archiv* discusses the preamble to the Czechoslovak-German Treaty, where the statement is made that "the Munich Agreement of 29th September 1938 is null and void" and that "the Czechoslovakia State had, since 1918, never ceased to exist". But, as the report notes, Slovakian politicians criticised these words claiming that this was not the case and in their opinion the Slovakian state established with

Hitler's help in March 1939 was a State that could not be challenged in international law. While the Slovakians (Hitler's fascist allies during the war) supported the Nazi division of the Czechs and the Slovaks as avidly as they support that same split today, the Bavarian Christian Social Union party and the Germans who used to live in the Sudetenland (but now for the most part live in Bavaria) also recognise as valid the actions of the Hitler regime which, by the Munich Agreement, annexed the Sudetenland to Germany. But they do not recognise what happened after that point — i.e. the break up of Czechoslovakia. The official German Government today sees in:

> ... the recognition of the invalidity of the (Munich) Agreement *from the beginning* retrospective problems for the treatment of the nationality of the Sudeten Germans.

Although the Czech Government does not accept there is any problem with the post war expulsions of Germans from Czechoslovakia (the then President Benes having justified the expulsions on the grounds that those expelled were German, not Czech citizens) the *Archiv* report notes that

> President Havel had emphasised on several occasions that expulsions without time limit he condemned in principle.

thus once again giving comfort to German concerns at the expense of legitimate Czech fears. Officially Prague sees the expulsions as no more than technical infringements of that "humane and ordered removal" which was regulated by the Potsdam Agreement. The Bavarian CSU complained that during the Treaty negotiations property formerly owned by Sudeten Germans was being auctioned. The Czech government pointed out that according to their law no claims could be made for property owned before 25th February 1948 (the Communist take-over) regardless of whether the claim came from a Czech, a Slovak, a German or any other nationality.

In other words the tensions over events before and during the Second World War exist today and so blight German-Czechoslovak relations that many of these issues were specifically excluded from the Treaty! For instance although it is quite clear to the Czechs and other European nations like the UK, Italy and France that the Munich Agreement was in international law "from the beginning null and void" President Havel noted that Germany "had its juridical reasons" why such a "formulation" could not be included in any treaty. Havel noted that "such a formulation would probably not be acceptable to the German Constitutional Court in Karlsruhe". Once again — as in countless other international agreements which Germany enters (like for instance the rights of parents over children or the extradition of German citizens, or German opt outs from the European Treaties) the German constitutional Court is used as an excuse not to obey the rules which German-signed treaties impose on other nations.

Despite the exclusion of articles unacceptable to the Czechoslovak Government, nevertheless, within the general framework of "human rights", "European citizenship", "cultural relations" etc the German side managed to include in this Czechoslovakia Treaty many provisions which could easily achieve what they could not spell out openly. For instance while article 2 commits both sides to "mutual recognition of borders, sovereignty and the non interference in internal affairs" Article 1 of the Treaty refers to both sides pursuing "a border free Europe of human rights". This could for instance allow Germans who say they are "European citizens" to claim their "human rights" to pursue their "cultural development" by re-acquiring the territory from which the Czechs have excluded them.

One of the methods of administrative conquest with which the British are becoming more familiar is the European Union's "regional principle" and here again in Article 13 of the German Czechoslovakian Treaty we see a commitment to "co-operation between regions and other local bodies". This is another deliberate attempt to break down the border between Germany and former "German" territory. Other well-trodden ways to "integration", especially through trans-national law, is evident in Article 17 — "common undertakings in environmental protection, in particular in common border regions" and in Article 18

— "Improvement in transport connections, extension of border crossings and ease of travel arrangements".

Article 20 is more open in its intentions — "Protection of the German Minority" in Czechoslovakia in particular "for those who declare their German culture and who can express that culture without discrimination; Czechoslovakia will make possible the promotion of the German minority by the German Federal Republic". Needless to say this seems an excessive degree of "interference in internal affairs" and is inconceivable in any "treaty" which for instance the British Government might negotiate with a foreign country. There follows a whole list of further methods whereby German cultural and in particular educational contacts will be promoted, in schools, universities, research, science, youth groups etc and is remarkably reminiscent of those "cultural" links established during the 1930s with the gullible in those nations subsequently invaded and destroyed.

Equally reminiscent of that period is the language used by Kohl on his visit to Czechoslovakia to sign the Treaty. Whereas Hitler had threatened Czechoslovakia with the railway analogy — that they had got on a train and it was not possible to get off because "the points were set" — so Kohl said:

> The Treaty is for us an expression of our relations as neighbours over centuries and also a setting of the points for future co-operation between our peoples. The Treaty starts from the central thesis that we can only build the future together if we together face the past. ... We must, as neighbours, put special weight on regional co-operation. In the border region between Bohemia (i.e. the Czechs) and Bavaria the Egerland has developed into a very promising example for cross border, neighbourly co-operation.

Kohl recalled the war years and the expulsion of the Sudeten Germans and sought to equate the wrongs done by both sides, a remarkable re-writing of history! He went on to say that the expelled Germans "want to be active in the development of Czechoslovakia" and in the following extract is clearly using the European Union yet again as a threat/enticement to "persuade" Czechs:

> ... we would welcome it if the Czechoslovak Government, in relation to its aspiring membership of the European union, would soon make it legally easier for foreigners to settle in Czechoslovakia.

In the forms of dominance sought by "German Europe" over the centuries, *plus ca change plus c'est la meme chose.*

7. VACLAV HAVEL — A CZECH PUPPET OF GERMAN EUROPE

In *The Irish Times* of 13th June the former Czech dissident and — until the end of his present term of office in 2003 — President of the Czech Republic, Vaclav Havel (born 1936), was interviewed by the paper's Foreign Affairs Correspondent. The interview demonstrated clearly the (at best) dangerous naivety of this disastrous Czech President.

Havel, with an international reputation in the resistance to the communist Soviet Union now kow-tows to the corporatism of the European Union. Havel, who succeeded in wresting democratic nationhood from the Soviet Superstate now wishes to surrender it to the European Union. Having fought the Russians military and economic imperialism he now embraces German industrial take-over and German Europe's hegemony. Havel, who was the first president of a free, post war Czechoslovakia, presided over the destruction of his own nation (by the recreation of Slovakia) and is now president of only the remnant "Czech Republic". No wonder he is not popular among real Czech democrats.

Havel is of course a romantic figure — a poet and dramatist turned political activist and he has been predictably seduced by romantic notions of a "United Europe" as a "truly functioning transparent, understandable organisation that brings benefit to all nations". Like many political dangermen he dreams of being part of a powerful imperialist superstate. He talks of a "region" "from Alaska in the West to Tallinn in the East" and "one of the components of a future multi-polar world order". During the 1930s and 1940s there were few terms with which European fascists were more happy than "The New World Order", reflecting as it does notions of power, global ambition, contempt for democratic nationhood and order (i.e. control).

Here we have the historical language of megalomania and fascism — from the lips of a romantic. No one who has the slightest knowledge of the foundation of the European Union, the methods of deceit used to establish its power, its destruction of free nations and democratic parliaments or its present corrupt reality could believe in its "benefits to all nations". But Havel does not live in the real world, he lives in the world of drama and poetry, just like the Nazis lived in the romantic greenery of the German countryside and in the heroic Wagnerian myths. Fundamentally weak figures always require big, powerful myths and big powerful States which can project their grand plans onto the wider world. Havel dreams of himself as the centre of attention when he recalls (with romantic historical anachronism) Bismarck's adage "Whoever controls Prague controls Europe"!

Well we know who controls Prague today. Through the Germanophile Havel, it is Berlin. Listen to how Dr Miroslav Polreich describes his attempts to negotiate a peace in Kosovo, (after the arming and training of Kosovo terrorists by the German Secret Service). Polreich was a former ambassador to the OSCE, who was on this first international peace mission to Pristina in Kosovo in 1992 under the leadership of David Peel the Canadian Ambassador.

> The Serbs were prepared to talk to anyone. If the other side wanted secrecy, OK, Rugova (Kosovo Albanian leader) had this condition. So I asked the authorities at the time and they told me "we consulted the Germans and they had no intention of having any kind of deal over Kosovo". Later I approached the authorities in Prague again offering my mandate from Rugova to go and negotiate — that was in the mid-1990s. They refused and said it was up to Havel.

So there were no negotiations. We were unable to help at the time when Kosovo was out of the media headlines and both sides were amenable to an agreement and the war could have been prevented. ... Somehow Germany is in power in Europe, economically, financially, in the media, the press ... absolutely, number one, no comparison.

And when it comes to the mundanities of the Nice Treaty — the latest building block in the German Europe project, Berlin can once again call on its puppet in Prague. This is part of a general tactic by the German State which was usefully used during the Austrian presidency (but which rather fell apart when Austria was "expelled" for the "extremism" of its democracy!). *The Irish Times* interview comes of course rather better from a Czech than a German and Havel was all too willing to play the part. Germany needed to put pressure on the Irish voters to approve the Nice Treaty but an overt German attempt would certainly backfire. In fact of course the Havel interview would have persuaded few people and the Irish rejected the treaty.

On the one hand Havel told *The Irish Times* that rejecting the Nice Treaty (which if he had read it has little to do with expansion and more with further concentrating undemocratic control over members states) would be like "Europe remaining divided — leaving a psychological remnant of the Iron Curtain". On the other hand he pours scorn on those who hark back to "times when there used to be blocs opposing each other". But of course Europe is not divided and therefore there is no need for the Czechs to give up their hard won sovereignty and democracy. And yet that is precisely what Havel urges them to do!

But why should there be any support for such a surrender of their democratic nationhood among Czechs, Hungarians and Poles? Because the Soviet-controlled barrier to the West has been replaced by the European Union's trade barriers to the East. The peoples of Eastern Europe do not wish to join the European union, they want to trade freely with the countries of Western Europe. It is the European Union which forcefully pre-

146

vents that, offering a removal of those barriers only when those eastern nations surrender their hard won nationhood and their national constitutions to the undemocratic institutions of the European Union.

Perhaps the most purblind of Havel's ludicrous beliefs is that the new European superstate would never "draw anybody into enmity against any adversary — that is no longer the case in the world today". This from a President of a country which has the closest affinity to the people of Yugoslavia, a country conspired against (by Germany) broken up, ethnically cleansed (largely by NATO), bombed (by NATO and the European Union) and suffering the deaths of 2,000 civilians in a war of unparalleled illegality. Following the break up of Yugoslavia, war and racial and religious bigotry (mainly from the Muslims and Croats whom NATO and German Europe supported) have led to further and continuing aggression in Croatia (which drove out 500,000 Serbs). Hundreds of thousands of Serbs have been driven out of Bosnia and Kosovo (the terrorist KLA, NATO's ally, being the chief "ethnic cleanser") and now Macedonia where the UN supported Kosovo Albanian militias have invaded — doubtless using the weaponry supplied by Germany, Belgium and other "peace loving countries". That is what Havel calls peace. We should be in no doubt what we should call Havel — the latest puppet of German Europe and a principal ingredient in the grave instability which threatens a wider war in Europe.

8. THE ILLEGALITY OF NATO'S AND GERMAN EUROPE'S WAR AGAINST YUGOSLAVIA

No single "achievement" of German Europe, under the guise of the "European Union", betrays the recreation of the 1930s and 1940s more than the destruction of the State of Yugoslavia. If the slippery ambiguities of modern eurofascism in the mouths of "moderate" politicians cleverly disguise their intent and the use of extra parliamentary methods like treaty law easily bamboozle members of parliament and if the "pragmatic" response to well nurtured crises allows the creation of more centralised power apparently in the name of "humanity" then the brutal, bloody break up of a sovereign nation with a (twice) elected head of state cannot be so easily disguised.

It is a tribute to the success of German Europe's entrapment of its former enemies in its well laid scheme that Britain, the United States and (to a lesser extent) France have turned on Yugoslavia — their historical ally in the European fight against European fascism — and destroyed it, demanding that in Bosnia peoples should live together in peace when Germany and NATO deliberately drove them apart in order to destroy multi-ethnic Yugoslavia!

There are many grounds for believing that NATO's (and the European Union's) war against Yugoslavia was illegal.

1. It was contrary to Chapter VII of the United Nations own charter since no specific UN authority was granted (NATO knew that the Russians and Chinese would veto any move to obtain such authority);

2. It was contrary to NATO's own charter which asserts that the alliance is purely defensive;

3. It was contrary to international law (and the Nuremberg trials definition of "aggressive war") in that the country attacked had not itself attacked any other country, but was merely defending its own territory — against the KLA in precisely the same way in which the United Kingdom has fought (with far more deaths) against the IRA in Northern Ireland.

4. It was in contravention of international law in that so-called "humanitarian assistance" cannot be used as an excuse for attacking a sovereign country (this was specifically established to counter Hitler's view that he had the right to invade Czechoslovakia).

5. The targeting of the Belgrade Television station and the deliberate killing of journalists was the most blatant example of NATO's illegality and about which the BBC

(as an apparently now legitimate target in future conflicts) is strangely unmoved.

6. Among those nations which acted illegally even from the
point of view of their own constitutions were Germany,
Italy and the United Kingdom (where no prior parliamentary approval for the war was sought or given).
Indeed even a House of Commons Committee subsequently admitted the illegality of the war.

7. The attempt, by threat of war, to force on Yugoslavia the
terms of the "Rambouillet Agreement" (which, in demanding effective free movement by NATO forces
throughout Yugoslavia, could never have been accepted
by any sovereign nation) was a blatant contravention of
the 1980 Vienna Convention on the Law of Treaties
which forbids the coercion of a state into signing an
agreement.

But today in a typical example of "victor's justice" it is Slobo-
dan Milosovic, the former twice elected leader of Yugoslavia
who sits before a Court in The Hague, specially constructed by
the NATO powers. Those who are trying Milosevic and who
committed the above illegalities have also been indicted but
they are not before the (real) International Court simply because they refuse to answer the summons!

But perhaps the most remarkable event since the end of the
Yugoslav war is a 1999 Berlin Appeal Court's description of
the NATO attack as "an illegal war", thus making NATO
leaders open to potential prosecution — both within and, more
significantly, without their own countries. This stance by a German court is all the more remarkable since it was the German
Intelligence Services which planned the break up of Yugoslavia
throughout the 1980s and supplied arms and support to Croat
Nationalists, Bosnian Muslims and Albanians in Kosovo and
Metohija. As in much else which has happened in Europe in
the 1980s and 1990s this German policy towards the Balkans is
an exact reprise of the policies of "German Europe" during the
1930s and 1940s (see below). Just as Germany, before the first

and the second world wars, intentionally sowed discontent among Croat and Albanian nationalists and religious bigots in order to weaken Serbia and Yugoslavia so today the only explanation of the present crisis is the resurgence of German Europe with its new plans for total integration of the free nations of Europe into a powerful and dangerous superstate.

Nevertheless in a court in Tiergarten in Berlin in May 1999 the judges found that by contributing to the NATO attack on Yugoslavia the German government and armed forces had in fact engaged in an illegal war. The implications for the leaders of the attack on Sovereign Yugoslav territory (Blair, Clinton, Schroder et al) are of course very serious.

The whole court case — and therefore the extraordinary condemnation of NATO leaders, including the German Chancellor Gerhard Schroeder, would never have come about had those who opposed the war attempted to take the German Government to court. But, unfortunately for the German (and British) political classes it was the German state prosecutor who started the whole legal process. The indictment of the Government resulted accidentally from the judgement of the court.

In an indictment of 2nd July 1999 the German State claimed that the accused (a total of 19 defendants) had distributed leaflets calling on others to commit an illegal act, namely desertion from the German armed services (Paragraph 16 Armed forces regulations) and the refusal to obey orders (Paragraph 20 of those regulations). In the edition of the newspaper the "Tageszeitung" of 21st April 1999 an advertisement had appeared in which the call to desert was published. I have translated the following extracts from the judgement of the Berlin Appeal court and it is as follows:

The accused confirmed that he had signed the call to desert. He had signed in the full knowledge and desire that it would be published widely. He knew that the advertisement would be published in the "Tageszeitung". He had only known of the distribution by mail by the witness H.T. when it was confirmed in the summons. Nevertheless he had without reservation fully en-

dorsed the distribution and had known when signing the call to desertion that it would come to such public exposure. He had not intended to call for illegal acts. On the contrary his intention had been to prevent soldiers committing illegal acts by attacking Yugoslavia. He had been convinced that a soldier could not commit an illegal act by following the call to desert.

The accused should be legally acquitted because that of which he was accused is not illegal. On neither count was there any call to an illegal act. ... An action is illegal (according to the German Legal Code) if it constitutes an offence under criminal law. This was not the case here. If the soldiers had followed the call to desert they would have been punishable neither for desertion nor for refusing to obey an order...because the use of the German armed services to attack the Federal Republic of Yugoslavia was an illegal act.

A soldier is not punishable if he refuses to take part in actions which are illegal under international law or absents himself from the forces in order to avoid participating in such actions. ... There is no obligation to obey if the orders which are disobeyed contravene the general provisions of international law.

This is of particular interest to those British and American airforce personnel who set off in their bombers to attack the civilians and journalists in the Belgrade television station. According to this German court judgement they could, indeed should have refused to do what Blair and Clinton ordered them to do. The judgement continues:

*This is particularly the case when the orders are issued within the context of an internationally illegal action. It does not depend on whether the issuing of the orders is seen by the issuer as a criminal wrongdoing since an order given which is contrary to international law need not be obeyed **even if the order is given for the best of motives.***

The Court asserted that the soldiers in question were to have absented themselves from their posts simply with the intention of avoiding participation in the armed attack on Yugoslavia.

There was no general encouragement to desert and abandoning one's post purely for the specific purpose of removing oneself from a particular action could only be punishable as desertion if that action was itself lawful said the court. The Court also considered whether the war against Yugoslavia was justified on the grounds of international law. It concluded that:

In so far as it is claimed that the action was justified by the fact that the UN was inactive or incapable of introducing measures under Chapter VII of the UN Charter, there are simply no facts which would justify such a claim. **The war was started without waiting for the passing of a resolution by the Security Council.**

The Court also rightly asserted that it could not be argued that the vetoing of a resolution justifying war by a permanent member of the UN (according to Article 27, Paragraph 3 of the UN Charter) could permit the other member States to bypass the Security Council and take the measures themselves. The Court also rejected a justification of the war on the grounds of emergency humanitarian relief, asserting that:

In any case there is the question as to whether humanitarian intervention in its original sense (military intervention by a State in order to rescue its own citizens abroad) would accord with international law. The war against Yugoslavia was not carried out to protect the citizens of the States which declared that war. It is also irrelevant to call on the occasionally quoted Article 51 of the UN Charter. The war was not pursued in order to support the Albanian population of Kosovo in its self-defence against human rights violations by the Yugoslavian State. Such a goal would have demanded the use of ground troops in the conflict but in fact the war was waged by means of air power against a part of Serb sovereign territory and its aim was to weaken the Federal Republic of Yugoslavia and thus force it to change its policy in Kosovo.

Indeed of course it was designed to wrest control and therefore at least *de facto* sovereignty over Kosovo from the state of Yugoslavia. This was made abundantly clear by the demands of the so-called Rambouillet Agreement, which amounted to effective surrender of Kosovo by Yugoslavia and was the kind of Agreement to which no nation state could possibly agree. We must remember that before the ethnic cleansing of Serbs by the KLA aided by NATO and before the ethnic cleansing through population growth by Albanians (whose families of 12 or 14 members are normal) and before the internal movement of Serbs by Tito (who was a Croat) and before the ethnic cleansing by Italian and German fascists during the war, the Serbs were never less than 50% of the population of Kosovo. The German court judgement continues:

An unauthorised intervention of this kind (i.e. NATO's attack on Yugoslavia) is, according to international law, illegal, even if it arises out of humanitarian motives. It contradicts the intention of the UN Charter according to which it is no longer permissible to conduct military solutions to international conflicts outside the institutional systems of collective security.

The judgement concludes:

The use of German armed forces against the Republic of Yugoslavia was objectively illegal since it was contrary to international law. ... The air war against the Federal Republic of Yugoslavia contravened the absolute prohibition of the use of military force by Article 2 Number 4 of the UN Charter. The prohibition applies to every form of military act which is used against the territorial integrity of another Sovereign State.

There is no doubt that Kosovo was (and still is) an integral part of the sovereign State of Yugoslavia and that it was the German supported and German supplied Kosovo Liberation Army which had waged war against the Government of Yugoslavia and which, with the help of NATO bombing and troops stationed in Kosovo after the war ethnically cleansed hundreds of thousands of Serbs from their own country. There is also little doubt about the massive *prima facie* evidence against the political leaders of the nations which participated in the NATO attack.

The so-called consensus of the "International Community" was of course no consensus at all with three of the world's major countries Russia, China and India categorically condemning the NATO attack. Similarly the ludicrous court established by NATO to put war criminals from the former Yugoslavia on trial (and incidentally the proposed International Criminal Court) have no credibility at all so long as the well-established cases against NATO leaders are so contemptuously dismissed. International courts before which we can never imagine our own leaders on trial are just not credible international courts. But perhaps like so many "rights" handed down to us (rather than the freedoms under the law which have always characterised the constitution and democratic rights of the British people), such "rights" are circumscribed and controlled by the political authority which grants them, not by objective law.

But we do have a system of international law which has arisen out of cases brought before various international and national courts. The Pinochet case demonstrated how even Heads of State who have contravened international law can be extradited from any state at the request of independent judges. Extradition Treaties signed by the British Government mean that only illness provides a possible way out of the inexorable legal process. Within Europe this process is even easier since the passage of the 1989 Extradition Act. Like Pinochet it might be advisable before venturing abroad for Messrs Blair, Clinton, Schroeder and Chirac to develop illnesses which could prevent their prosecution. Otherwise they may be invited to appear before the courts of any country which might take a different view of what constitutes a "war crime".

9. YUGOSLAVIA AND ITS ENEMIES 1903 - 1998

"We were escorted by a woman from the US Embassy as we flew towards Tusla. She pointed at all the destroyed villages and exclaimed excitedly 'Look at what the criminal Serbs have done'. In fact they were Bosnian Croat villages ethnically cleansed by the Muslims ... Later (we) visited Mostar where the Croats had virtually destroyed the Muslim sector. The US offi-

cial cried: 'Well at least this was done by the criminal Serbs.'
The woman burst into tears when it was pointed out that the
Croats had been to blame." General Sir Michael Rose, former
UN Military Commander in Bosnia, interview with *The Times*
10th November 1998

1. 1903 - 1918

Austria-Hungary, the last Catholic Empire, in decline.
Catholicisation of Dalmatia and Slavonia. The creation of
"greater Croatia". The Slav revolution — Serbia as the centre
of resistance to Austria-Hungary and seen by the Vatican as the
westernmost outpost of the hated "schismatic Slavdom".

1905 — The Tariff War: Austria-Hungary blockade of Serbia.

1908 — Austria-Hungary annexes Bosnia-Herzegovina and the
Serbs in Bosnia become victims of cultural and religious persecution.

1909 — Zagreb: Austria-Hungary puts Serbs on trial for "high
treason".

> "Archduke Franz Ferdinand (of Austria Hungary) wished to
> stem the advance of Orthodox Christianity by converting the
> largest possible number of Serbs to Roman Catholicism.
> The Archduke suggested to Brosch that they should all (i.e.
> Orthodox, Catholic and Muslims) be dropped into a caul-
> dron and only the Catholics should be allowed to come to
> the surface." — *Die Aussenpolitik Franz Ferdinands* by Le-
> opold Lumetzky, Berliner Monatshefte, June 1944 p. 187.

1914 —Serbia blamed for assassination of Franz Ferdinand (in
fact the assassin Gavrilo Princip (1895-1918), born in Bosnia,
was a citizen of Austria-Hungary, not Serbia).

ALBANIA

1913 — Albania was an artificial creation by Germany and Austria- Hungary in order to block Serbia's access to the Adriatic. (compare German domination of Albania today and its funding and arming of the Albanian KLA against Serbia)

1913 —Serbian troops are warned by Austria-Hungary and Germany not to pursue the gangs of Albanian terrorists across the border into Albania. (1998 NATO, driven by "German Europe", threatens Serbia for defending its own territory — KOSOVO — from where most Serbs were driven out by the Nazis during the Second World War.

1914 — The Vatican gives wholehearted support to Austria-Hungary's attack against Serbia. Austria-Hungary's campaign of hatred against the Serbs. Croatian and Muslim hooligans embark on mass pogrom against the Serbs throughout Croatia and Bosnia — supported by official propaganda. (1989 President Tudjman of Croatia describes genocide as a "natural phenomenon, it is not only permitted it is commended indeed it is commanded by the Almighty in defence of the only true faith (i.e. Catholocism)". 1990 — Tudjman's Ustasha thugs return from abroad (mainly Germany) to Croatia to attack Serbs. Tudjman decrees that Serbs are "an alien minority" — 40,000 flee).

1914 —The Catholic Bishops bless the arms of the Croat, Muslim and Slovenian recruits. Dr Marko Natlacen, prominent Slovenian clerical politician published a poem "String up the Serbs".

1915 — Horrific bombardment of Belgrade by German artillery. 400,000 tons of steel fell on the city in just 4 days. Austria- Hungary's reign of terror, tens of thousands of Serb civilians murdered. Unsuccessful attempt by the occupying force to convert the Serbian population to Catholicism. (Compare their "success" of force converting 244,000 Serbs between 1941 and 1944!)

1917 — When Catholic Austria-Hungary was evidently about to fall, the Vatican sought to shore up the defences against Orthodoxy. Bishop Jeglich of Lubljana and the "Superior General" of the Jesuits, General Halke von Ledochowsky tried to create a Slav Catholic empire. The Ledochowsky Plan became an obsession of Pius XII. A similar plan was put to Clemenceau in 1918 by Josef Retinger, the Jesuit intriguer and founder of the European Movement and the Bilderberg group. For such intrigues, mainly on behalf of the Vatican, Retinger was expelled from allied countries during the First World War.

(1998, with the help of the German Foreign Office, the Austrian Cultural Institute in London organised a month long festival of "Central European Culture" — the participant countries being predominantly Catholic.)

1918 - 1945

Deliberate attempt by the Vatican to prevent creation of the new Kingdom of Serbs, Croats and Slovenes in the new Independent Yugoslavia. (Contrast haste with which the Vatican was the first state to recognise Nazi Germany in 1933 and Slovenia, Croatia and Bosnia in the 1990s!)

1929 — Pius XI and Mussolini's Roman Empire

> "Bishops took an oath of allegiance to the fascist dictatorship and the clergy were ordered never to oppose it or incite their flock to harm it. Prayers were said in churches for Mussolini and for fascism. Priests became members of the Fascist Party and were even among its officers"
> *The Vatican's Holocaust*, A. Manhattan Ozark Books, Springfield, USA 1986

Nuns parade through Rome on the back of open lorries giving the Fascist salute to the Mussolini regime. (Archive Film)

Cardinal Pacelli (the future Pius XII) mission in Berlin — the strengthening of the bond between German Imperialism and Catholic expansionism. First aim to convert Prussia to Catholicism. Future Pope's fascination with Germany. A close friend of the Vatican was Ante Pavelic, leader of the Croatian fascist

"Ustasha" the military backing for the forced conversions, persecution and killing of Serbs.

1934 — An Ustasha (Croatian Fascists) -trained terrorist assassinates King Alexander I of Yugoslavia in Marseilles. The King had been invited by the French Government to discuss measures for countering the aggressive foreign policy of Nazi Germany.

The rise of clericalism in Yugoslavia:

> "Franciscan schools in Sinj, Siroki Brijeg and Visoko, seminaries in Makarska, Mostar and Split and the theological faculty in Zagreb were the centres of national consciousness, that is, nests from which flocks of priests and toilers in God's vineyard took off every year as well as flocks of national fighters, teachers of national Ustasha consciousness."
> Zagreb weekly, "The Independent State of Croatia", 1941, issue 33, page 42.

> "I know you were among those who did not hesitate or doubt, among those who acted."
> Ante Pavelic, speech to Croatian Crusaders of 19.6.1941, Catholic Weekly, Sarajevo 20.8.41.

> "Your actions played a significant role in our political struggle."
> Ante Pavelic speech to the representatives of Catholic Action, 21.6.1941.

1930s — Franz Neuhausen and his German intelligence net in Yugoslavia (exact parallels of Germany's secret service in 1980s Yugoslavia.

Pope Pius XII blesses Mussolini's troops at their entry into the Second World War.

1941 — Serbs reject Yugoslavia becoming part of Axis powers. Goebbels propaganda Blitzkrieg — Serbs accused of pillaging and ethnic cleansing (by Goebbels!!) Compare exactly the same methods of "German Europe" in the 1990s.

NAZI INVASION 6th April 1941. Belgrade, previously declared an open City, bombed by Luftwaffe, 30,000 civilians die.

1941 (10th April) — German army enters Zagreb and *de facto* creates the "Independent State of Croatia", which became puppet Nazi State ruled by Pavelic and his Ustasha thugs. Croat priests aided by Ustasha forced Orthodox Serbs to convert at the point of a gun to Roman Catholicism. Unleashed the most horrifying religious massacre of the 20th century — *circa* 1million Serbs murdered between 1941 and 1945. JASENOVAC concentration camp where between 400,000 and 700,000 were murdered (90% Serbs, the rest Jews and gypsies).

"I must admit that I have been obsessed with the criminal character of the Independent State of Croatia. Even the Germans were appalled by the crimes committed in it."
Simon Wiesenthal, 1990 interview with Yugoslav magazine "NIN".

"The greatest genocide in World War II in proportion to a nation's population took place not in Nazi Germany but in the Nazi-created Independent State of Croatia. There, in the years 1941-1945 some 750,000 Serbs, 60,000 Jews and 26,000 gypsies perished in a gigantic holocaust."
French historian Edmond Paris, from *Genocide in Satellite Croatia 1941-1945*, Melbourne 1981

The Vatican's role in the persecution of Serbs and non-Catholics: FORCED CONVERSIONS:

"Special offices and church committees must be created immediately for those to be converted ... Let every curate remember that these are historic days for our mission and we must under no circumstances let this opportunity pass. (i.e. the fascist control of Yugoslavia). Our work* is legal because it is in accord with official Vatican policy and with the directives of the Saintly Congregation of the Cardinals for the Eastern Church."
From "The Voice of the Archbishopric of Krizevci", issue 2 1942. The author is the Apostolic Administrator and Bishop

of Krizevci, Dr Janko Shimrak, a close colleague of Archbishop Stepinac beatified by the Pope in October 1998!

* This "work" consisted of promising terrorised Serbs (often whole villages) that their lives would be spared if they "returned" to "the true faith" — Roman Catholicism. Mass (forced) conversion "ceremonies" were conducted by Catholic monks accompanied by detachments of Ustasha troops.

"The Papal legate in Croatia, Mgr Marcone, openly blessed the Ustasha and publicly gave the fascist salute."

"In an official document dated as late as May 8th 1944 His Eminence Archbishop Stepinac, head of the Catholic hierarchy (in Nazi Croatia) informed the Holy Father that to date '244,000 Orthodox Serbs have been converted to the Church of God'."

"The Schism (the Orthodox Church) is Europe's greatest curse, almost greater than Protestantism. It knows no morals, principles, truth, justice or decency." Diaries of Archbishop Stepinac, Volume 4, p. 176, Entry 28.3.1941.

All quotations from A. Manhattan, *The Vatican's Holocaust*, op cit.

1940s — Break up of Yugoslavia into ethnic groups under the Nazis. Yugoslavs were split into about 12 different racial and religious states. The German WAFFEN SS divisions were organised according to such racial and ethnic divisions and included:

HANDZAR — the Bosnian Muslims

KAMA — the Croats

SKENDERBEG — Albanians

PRINZ EUGEN — Yugoslavia's Ethnic Germans

"However unsavoury the reputation of these SS units, there were individuals eager to recreate the SS Handzar division under a slightly different name in the 1990s. The 13th Waffen SS was dropped and an organisation of the veterans of the World War 2 Handzar division was founded in Sarajevo (early 1990s). It seems that the first attempt to recreate a unit called 'Handzar Division' was launched in Sisak, Croatia in the early 1990s."

"More recently a Handzar division surfaced under the operational control of the Bosnian Government. One of its duties is to protect President Izetbegovic."

The Bully on the Block: American Policy in the Former Yugoslavia, by Ivan Avakumovic, The University of British Columbia (1996)

1943 —Otto von Habsburg travels to the USA to lobby Congress for the creation of a "Danube Monarchy" - i.e. the revival of the Ledochowsky plan.

THE VATICAN AND ITS "RATLINES"

Thousands of Catholic war criminals were shielded from justice after the Second World War and were actively assisted by the Holy See.

"I gather that...some arrangement has been worked out with the Vatican and Argentina. ... protecting not only Quislings but also those guilty of terrible crimes committed in Yugoslavia. I presume we must protect our agents even though it disgusts me ... we are conniving with the Vatican and Argentina to get guilty people to haven in the latter country."

John Moors Cabot, US Ambassador to Belgrade June 1947 (From *Ratlines*)

Kurt Waldheim (UN Secretary General 1972-81, Chancellor of Austria 1986-92) — a personal link between the past and the present, Nazism and Yugoslavia and Nazism and the Vatican. Waldheim was the first statesman to be visited by the newly elected and extremist leaders of Croatia and Bosnia in 1990.

1942 — Waldheim was awarded one of the highest Croatian decorations — the "Zvonimir Medal with Oak Leaves" by Ante Pavelic, the Croatian fascist leader.

"Continuing his research, Herzstein found a captured German activity report for July 1942 that summarised the medals awarded in connection with the Kozara operation (massacres) ... 139 decorations, including the 'wounded badge' were handed out among the twenty thousand troops who took part. And only two German soldiers were awarded the 'Zvonimir medal with Oak Leaves'." *Betrayal*, by Eli M. Rosenbaum, St Martins Press, New York 1993 P 123

"Waldheim is usually the only guest at the fund raiser for Friends of the Waffen SS." (*The Observer Magazine*, 19.8.1988)

1948 — Yugoslav Government named Waldheim as a war criminal. He was never prosecuted. Despite the opposition of the World Jewish Congress Waldheim became Secretary General of the UN and then Chancellor of Austria. The Croatian Nationalist Krajacic (then a high ranking party and government official) was the major defender of Waldheim in Yugoslavia as well as the chief conduit for the German secret service campaign to destabilise Yugoslavia in the 1980s. It was in the late 1980s that Waldheim held regular meetings with Kohl, Genscher and Klaus Kinkel (head of German Secret Service from 1980) at a spa near Salzburg:

"During his frequent summer holidays in Austria Kohl often met Waldheim privately." *Neue Zurcher Zeitung*, 29.3.1992

1994 — The Pope awards Waldheim the highest decoration of the Roman Catholic Church.

1945 - 1991

The conspiracy of silence — the campaign by the Vatican to exonerate Pius XII and Cardinal Stepinac (the leading Catholic figure in Ustasha-ruled Croatia during the second world war) to suppress the truth about fascist Croatia.

The post war failure of denazification. In Germany US General Lucius Clay curtails industrial and political denazification programme. Acceptance by Albert Speer's US interrogators of too much of the Nazi version of "building Europe".

Early **1960s** — German Secret Service starts gradual process of infiltrating and undermining the State of Yugoslavia.

1966 — The removal by Marshall Tito of Aleksander Rankovic, the Serbian Head of the Yugoslav Secret Service signalled the beginning of infiltration of State institutions by Croatian and Muslim Separatists.

1974 — Bosnian Muslims become a nation. They were in fact Slavs but were given separate nation status solely on grounds of religion — a blueprint for the same logic to be applied to Croatia.

1981 — German Intelligence Service war against Yugoslavia enters a new aggressive phase with the appointment of Klaus Kinkel as Director General. Over a hundred agents of the German Secret Service sent into Yugoslavia.

1989 — The fall of the Berlin Wall — the rise of the new German-European Empire — based on the mythology of Charlemagne (crowned in Rome AD 800) and the "Holy Roman Empire of the German Nation". German re-unification despite the resistance of France and Britain. (The French agreed on the condition that they would have major influence on the future European Central Bank — Germany recently went back on that tacit agreement). In Britain Mrs Thatcher's doubts were swept aside by Douglas Hurd *et al.*

Hans Dietrich Genscher, the German Foreign Minister and Yugoslavia:

> "Germany's pro-Croat policy was heavily influenced by Croats who voted in Germany and who had hitherto preferentially voted for Genscher's Liberal Party (FDP)."

"In their hearts the Germans were always in favour of lifting the arms embargo for the Croats and by extension for the Muslims."
Balkan Odyssey, by David Owen, Victor Gollancz, London 1995.

"By recognising Croatia in December 1990 against the will of other members of the European Union the USA and Russia, German Foreign Minister Hans-Dietrich Genscher made it clear that Germany's interest in establishing a zone of influence in the Adriatic was sufficiently strong to risk creating serious divisions within NATO."
Der Schattenkrieger, by E. Schmidt-Eenboom, Econ Verlag, Dusseldorf.

1990 — THE DESTRUCTION OF YUGOSLAVIA

Germany, Belgium and Austria arm and support the Croatian and Slovenian separatists. Zagreb pop song "Danke Deutschland". Jasenovac Memorial — Tudjman's attempt to re-write history.

Britain gives way to German pressure to recognise Croatia and Slovenia — the "Maastricht Trade-off" (see Owen, Kaufman). A good example of how "German Europe" (by binding Britain into economic dependence on European Treaties) has fatally weakened British power to pursue traditional "balance of power" and pro national democracy policies in Europe.

1993 — Rudolf Augstein, managing editor of the "left liberal" German weekly *Der Spiegel* calls for "the decimation of the Serb civilian population". (*Der Spiegel* 18/1993) Germany's effective take-over of Albania. Germany a haven for Kosovo Liberation Army members. Otto von Habsburg calls for the bombing of Belgrade. A classic demonstration of how the Left and the Right in Germany and Austria combine, as they did in fascist Europe of the 1930s and 1940s, to promote "German Europe's" historic ambitions.

CROATIA becomes one of the most ethnically pure states in the world. A State just for Croats in which Serbs are categorised by the extremist President of Croatia Franjo Tudjman as an "alien minority". (Both Serbs and Croats speak Serbo-Croat!).

"The first refugees in the Yugoslav conflict were the 40,000 Serbs who fled Croatia after a constitutional amendment defined them as an alien minority." Simon Wiesenthal reported by Reuters.

1995 — OPERATION "STORM" — NATO aided expulsion of 300,000 Serbs from the KRAJINA.

"Washington gives tacit support to Croat attack" — *The Times* 4.8.1995.

"The close links between the USA and Croatia were symbolised by Peter Galbraith, the American Ambassador in Zagreb, who posed for photographs on top of a Croat tank prior to the Croat offensive in West Slavonia in May 1995." *The Bully on the Block* by Ivan Avakumovic

THE ISLAMIC ATTACK ON YUGOSLAVIA:

"There can be no peace or co-existence between the Islamic faith and non-Islamic institutions ... The Islamic movement must and can take power as soon as it is morally and numerically strong enough, not only to destroy the non-Islamic power but to build up a new Islamic one ... Turkey, as an Islamic country, used to rule the world. Turkey as an imitation of Europe, represents a third rate country."
The Muslim Declaration by Alija Izetbegovic (President of Bosnia and NATO's ally in the war against Yugoslavia) Sarajevo 1969

1995 — The Bosnian Muslim bombing of their own people in the market place of Sarajevo in order to try to blame the Serbs (later revealed by the UN as a well constructed lie). The incident led to a NATO ultimatum and subsequent bombing of Serbs.

FROM 1996 — In order to provoke retaliation by the Serbs, which could then lead to NATO and UN attacks on Serbia, German civil and military intelligence trained and equipped the Kosovo Liberation Army, harboured the so-called government of the "Kosovo Republic in exile" in Germany, set up one of its largest secret service stations in the Albanian capital Tirana, selected recruits for the KLA command structure, provided them with communications equipment and weapons and smuggled weapons from the former East Germany for use in Kosovo.

This created a serious rift between the German Secret Service and the American CIA. Nevertheless the western powers accepted uncritically the farce of Germany both secretly whipping up the conflict and then joining "peace keeping forces".

By accepting "German Europe's" propaganda about Yugoslavia the Foreign Office, some elements in the US Government and the British Press in general turned our historical enemies into friends and historical allies into enemies. Our friends looked on in disbelief and our enemies cheered us on. Britain thereby weakened the anti fascist forces on the continent, attacked national democracies, enhanced the power of the new Eurostate and broke up non racial nations into many racial or religious statelets — just as the Nazis did during the war and just as German Europe welcomes today.

The recent history of Yugoslavia is the clearest and most extreme example of *Europe's Full Circle* — back to the worst days of the 1930s and 1940s. Yugoslavia's enemies are also Britain's enemies — then as now.

10. THE CRISIS IN EUROPE AND THE THREAT TO THE UNITED STATES

A version of the following was originally written as a separate paper for American politicians and policy advisers:

The European Union, which American business sees as an opportunity and American politicians see as a contribution to European peace and security, is in fact the greatest danger to world peace today. It is a precise reproduction (in word, political structures, political philosophy and aims) of that obnoxious mixture of German imperialism and continental fascism which Britain and America defeated in two world wars.

The United Kingdom effectively no longer exists. The Westminster Parliament is subordinate to the European Commission in Brussels whose 30,000 plus regulations simply bypass it and whose directives instruct it. The British Courts must answer to the superior European Court of Justice in Strasbourg which has declared it has a *political* task — to further the "integration" (i.e. abolition) of the once free nation states of Europe. In other words it is not a court in any Anglo-Saxon sense of the word but every day it makes unrepealable law for 15 "nations". British people can now be extradited to any European country without the protection of *habeas corpus* or trial by jury. German citizens cannot be extradited anywhere! (This lack of symmetry is remarkably similar to the French surrender terms in 1940). The recent Nice Treaty makes it possible for the European Union to ban political parties of which it does not approve.

In 1991 Germany, followed rapidly by the Vatican, recognised Croatia, the most murderous state for its size during the fascist period. Croats massacred one million Serbs, gypsies and Jews mainly at the Jasenovac concentration camp between 1941 and 1945. The wartime Archbishop Stepinac whose own priests helped to run the extermination camp and carried out forced conversions of Orthodox Christians to Catholocism was recently beatified by the Pope.

In Eastern Europe the agricultural economy has collapsed, not least because the European Union severely restricts their exports to the West, and their media, business and agricultural land are being acquired by western European business, especially German firms. Just as Nazism planned in the 1930s, the nation states of Europe, for whose freedom Britain and America fought two bloody wars, effectively no longer exist as self-governing entities. American Foreign Policy has encouraged or ignored what the so-called "European Union" has caused:

- the destruction of 15 democratic nations,

- the abolition of 12 currencies and central banks,

- 16 million unemployed (due to preparation for the EURO),

- the break up of Czechoslovakia, the destruction of Yugoslavia,

- ethnic cleansing of a million Serbs,

- attacks on Jews and gypsies in Slovakia and Kosovo,

- synagogues and Turkish homes burned in Germany,

- threats to Norway and Switzerland unless they join the European Union,

- the re-creation of former Nazi puppet states (Slovenia, Croatia, Slovakia)

- threats against Poland, the Czech Republic and Britain, German expansion Eastwards

- a barrier to the democratic integration of former Soviet satellites into the free world

Even before the recent treaties of Amsterdam and Nice further consolidated its Europe-wide power, Germany was able to:

- turn Britain and America against its historical ally in the fight against German imperialism and fascism - Yugoslavia,

- inveigle itself through massive loans to a bankrupt Russia into an embryo Molotov Ribbentrop pact (probably based on secret bilateral agreements in the 80s and 90s)

- using "negotiations" of past treaties (like Maastricht) to turn a 11 to 1 opposition to the break up of Yugoslavia into an "EU policy" which did just that,

- while tying down other EU countries into a "common" foreign policy, pursue ruthlessly its bullying of Poland and The Czech Republic,

- used EU trade barriers against Eastern Europe and the prospect of NATO membership to entice east European countries into the European Union.

- used Russian fears of that very NATO expansion to seduce Yeltsin/Putin away from the USA and Britain towards a new Franco- Russian-German axis.

KALININGRAD AND THE ALIENATION OF THE RUSSIANS

The case of the Russian enclave now cut off from Russia by the independent Baltic states — Kaliningrad (formerly Koenigsberg, the centre of historic Prussia) is a classic case of the German use of the European Union and massive loans to Russia in order to achieve expansion eastwards.

The irresponsibly high levels of loans lavished on Russia by the German State and by the German banks (guaranteed by the German State) are both a source of great instability for the Russian economy and the basis of their increasing political dependence on German goodwill — as indeed they were designed to be. Helmut Kohl calculated that any threat from a financially naive Russia to hold German banks to ransom (i.e. refusing to repay debts) would be a step too far and might alienate the whole of western capital on which the rebuilding of the Russian economy depends.

There are already discussions on the conversion of German debt into equity stakes in Russian companies and the commissioner responsible for the European Union's external affairs, Chris Patten (a political reject from the United Kingdom) has made, in the words of The Times, the first steps in discussing the possible "political status of Kaliningrad in an enlarged Europe". Under the further disguise of the Swedish presidency of the European Union in the first six months of 2001 no doubt Germany's historical foreign policy aims and German industry's expansion will once again, as in the Balkans, be conveniently pursued under the cover of "a united Europe".

There remain now mere "mopping up" operations. The final steps in the creation of that corporatist, anti democratic, anti nation state power based on German Europe are the EURO (Britain, Sweden, Denmark, Norway and Switzerland remain outside, the latter two are not even in the European Union) and the European Army (now in embryo form and the greatest threat to United States interests).

"We do not have the feeling that we are an inferior race. Some worthless pack that can be kicked around ... we are a great Volk which only once forgot itself." — Adolf Hitler June 1934, Gena.

"Germany has every interest in considering itself a great power in Europe (which must have) a foreign policy of fully acknowledged self interest." NATO "served to protect Germany but also as a protection against Germany. This concept no longer has value." — German Chancellor Schroeder, German Unions Monthly Review, September 1999.

Very little seems to have changed in 60 years. Indeed it was precisely the impossibility of distinguishing between Hitler's ambitions and the "normal" German political class in the 1930s which led the British Foreign Office to break off negotiations with von Trott, the then great hope of conservative "good Germans" overthrowing Hitler. Writers today in Britain (myself, a Conservative) Sweden (Jan Myrdal, a socialist) and others in Yugoslavia, Poland and Czechoslovakia warn of these dangerous parallels today because there are inherent imperial ambitions and a strong tendency to corporatist/anti-democratic beliefs even in the (apparently) non extreme elements in German politics.

THE CATASTROPHIC EFFECTS OF GERMAN EUROPE ON US FOREIGN POLICY

Never has foreign policy been so critical to an American Administration. The corporatist and protectionist European Union has prevented the true acceptance of the former Soviet satellites into the world community of free trade and democracy (the former is denied them now, their parliamentary democracies would be denied them on entry into the "European" Union, a construction which represents a mere one third of the nations of Europe).

The Yugoslav war has revealed to Slavs, orthodox Christians, eastern Europeans (and in particular the NATO member Greece) an aggressive, German-dominated "West" whose embrace they now shun. During the second world war the true measure of the intentions of the German Reich was not to see the relatively chivalrous way in which the Nazi authorities treated imprisoned Allied officers (this writer's father was a witness to that) but the way in which they treated the "subhuman", the Slavs, the orthodox and the Eastern Europeans. While the easily mollified "West" has not even woken up to the reality of 21st century German power politics the Russians and their allies in the East need no reminding and see clearly the true nature of "German Europe".

The Yugoslav war showed the Russians that they cannot trust the West. Yeltsin warned the British and the Americans that the attack on Yugoslavia would seriously affect the whole of East-West relations for decades to come. Putin and Yeltsin warned that NATO expansion eastwards (driven more by German Europe as a means of expanding the European Union than by the US and UK) would in Putin's words be "a mistake and we say it is unacceptable". Putin also summed up the effects of the (German inspired) Balkan crisis "Our relations with the West have moved backwards since the events in the Balkans." It is therefore not surprising that the Russians have decided to re-establish their armed strength, their renewed links with their former satellites, the suppression of national sovereignty (Chechnya and Georgia) — and even their links with Castro.

In Eastern Europe and in the Caucasus the Russian Bear is reacting to German Europe's Expansionism by using the same tactics against smaller nations in the east as Germany is doing in West and central Europe — i.e. establishing (or in the case of Russia trying to re-establish a quasi soviet block) an imperial power over historic and non racial nations by promoting racial and religious statelets within them and economic, bureaucratic, supranational blocks above them.

China has been permanently alienated. Communist revanchistes throughout Eastern Europe and in China have been given ample ammunition to re-establish their hegemony. Aggressive German Europe has united Conservatives, Liberals, socialists and even communists in opposition to it. We see the re-creation of that alliance which was last seen during the 1930s and 1940s — the last time communists were regarded, even by non communists, as "being right".

THE SOLUTION

The George W. Bush administration must not disengage from Europe. Bush will have to try to remedy the disastrous consequences of both Clinton's *disengagement* and his naive and historically dangerous *interventions* during the 1990s. The recent extraordinary manipulations by the French and Germans to create in the so-called "European Rapid Reaction Force" an alternative to NATO has brought home to Americans at last the kind of Europe that successive US presidents have deliberately and

172

naively constructed and which now represents a grave threat to US interests.

British doubts about the US missile shield, increasing trade friction, the Kyoto "Agreement" and of course the rapid Reaction Force have sharpened trans-Atlantic tensions and shown the vacillation of the Europhile Blair regime, seeking to maintain the "special relationship" and all the shared military and intelligence resources on the one had while promoting Blair's personal image as a "European leader" on the other.

"We think the Rapid Reaction Force is nothing other than a European Army — a counter to NATO" said one Washington Official. On missile defence a member of the Administration said of the Blair Government's doubts "You're either with us or you're not." One "observer close to Vice president Cheney" as the British journalist put it said:

> We trust you because of our history, our culture, our interests. But if you jump into bed with the French and the Germans you can kiss goodbye to all that. Why would we share information with you if it then goes to the who would hand it over to Iraq or the Germans who would fax it to Teheran. (The Germans provided the Iranians with one of the world's most powerful computers for their Intelligence Services)

But it was US Presidents from Kennedy to Clinton, with few exceptions who encouraged and helped to construct the European Union which in turn alienated the historic, economic, strategic and cultural ties between the Anglo Saxon nations. If today the British political class faces one way, its people another and the USA is confused by British loyalties, then Americans are observing a disaster of their own making.

In the recent past it was the administration of George Bush Senior, which fatally started to listen more to German rather than to British views of Europe. The catastrophic weakness of the John Major years, the Conservative Party's use of in intelligence files on Clinton, the capture of most of the British political establishment by Eurocorporatism and the gradual destruction of the British constitution mean of course that Britain is more to blame than the USA.

But the two critical periods of euro-corporatist influence on Britain (rightly seen throughout Europe by anti-fascist forces as the sole pillar of democratic nationhood) were directed through Washington — the Kennedy/Macmillan years and the Clinton/Blair years. The Reagan/Thatcher period was an interlude of sanity, brought to an end by the machinations of those corporatist cliques typified by Bilderberg gatherings (Margaret Thatcher was dismissed not by the electorate or by the Conservative Party but by corporatist cliques on her own back benches.

Too many senior politicians on both sides of the Atlantic have been regular attendees at meetings of the Bilderberg group, but even many of them are slowly accepting the malign influence of that organisation and realise what is really happening in Europe. Bilderberg, according to the CIA's Richard Aldrich, was the prime mover in the creation of the European Union as it is today and was even more significant than the European Movement. Two notorious anti-nation activists founded Bilderberg. (see the books *Europe's Full Circle* and *Treason at Maastricht* for more on the Bilderberg Group)

1. Prince Bernhard of the Netherlands, the former German Prinz zur Lippe Biesterfeldt, SS Intelligence officer attached to the Nazis main industrial supporter, I G Farben, member of the Nazi party from 1933 up to his marriage into the Dutch royal family in 1937. Resigned after intimate involvement in the Lockheed scandal.

2. Joseph Retinger, a Vatican agent of influence, ejected from allied countries during the first world war for plotting a central Europe Catholic empire. He never carried a national passport (he was Polish) and founded the European Movement in 1946. He believed in "working behind the scenes" to abolish the nations of Europe.

When attacked by Bilderberg, Margaret Thatcher said she regarded it as a compliment! How right she was. But there are many positive signs of a fight back against the evils listed above:

1. Activists like myself (censored by most of the British press) have nevertheless succeeded over the last 10 years in turning public opinion against the European Superstate — 51% of the British people now wish to leave the European Union, 70% oppose the EURO.

2. British industry, having been the leading proponents of the European Union, now largely opposes the abolition of the pound for the EURO. British agriculture, initially "bought" by European subsidies, has now been decimated by the soviet style "common agricultural policy" and now largely opposes the European Union.

3. There are increasingly strong non-extreme anti-Eurostate movements throughout Europe.

4. The Euro has been a disaster and the crunch — necessary fiscal centralism (see the recent attack on the elected Government of Ireland by the European Central Bank) — is about to expose the inherent conflict between national parliaments and the Brussels State.

THE BUSH REGIME MUST HELP AND ENCOURAGE THESE MOVEMENTS BY:

1. Giving no support either political or monetary to the EURO. Continue to exclude nations in the EURO from separate representation at the IMF etc.

2. Giving overt support (including encouraging private funding) to the respectable anti EU movements in Britain and Europe (caution required). Give the anti-EU movement recognition and the status of communication with the US Administration.

3. Beware of and prevent excessive Russian reliance on German loans, which are used as a political weapon (see Kalining-

rad question) and a source of take-over of Russian industry. The British and American governments should offer alternative sources of capital to Russia (see 7. below).

4. Use the WTO to break down the trade barriers between East and West Europe, thus breaking down "fortress Europe" behind which the EU dispenses trade "privileges" in return for democratic constitutional surrender.

5. Create a world-wide free trading group based on the US, UK, Ireland and the British Commonwealth (accounts for 40% of world trade compared to 20% for the European Union).

6. Then create an "umbrella" between that trade area and the new nations of Eastern Europe, bypassing the European Union, and allowing the freedoms of democracy and trade to reach — at last — those nations the allies freed from Soviet and Nazi slavery.

7. Reduce inter-state and bank finance for Russia, instead encourage free trade and western entrepreneurial skills and private (and personal) equity.

8. Support the British government when it resists European "integration" and support withdrawal from the constitutional structures of the European Union — this is what the British parliament and British people voted for in, respectively, 1972 and 1975.

9. Beware of German pressure on Eastern Europe. Criticise and act against German attempts to force treaties on Poland and the Czech Republic.

10. Beware German links with China and French links with Iraq. Make the French pay a price for their chauvinism and anti-Anglo- Saxon activities (including spying)

11. *Never* let the US/British/New Zealand/Canada/Australia intelligence links be shared with the European Union.

12. Insist on obedience to UN resolutions since 1970s by Israel - thus preventing world-wide Islamic attacks on the West. Re-

member German activities in Iraq in the 1920s and the vast supply of German chemical factories to Iraq in the 1980s and the evidence from an Iraqi defector (BBC programme "Correspondent" 3rd March 2001) that Germany contributed 80% of the resources needed to establish the Iraqi nuclear weapons programme. Note also the German encouragement of Bosnian and Albanian Muslims in the break up of Yugoslavia.

13. Give top priority to re-assuring Russia and Greece of the US resistance to a German-dominated European Union expanding eastwards.

14. Do not recognize "Europe" only the "free nations of Europe trading in a free world".

15. Stop the European Rapid Reaction Force, or at the very least prevent it planning or operating outside NATO structures or outside Europe.

CHAPTER 5

A SOVEREIGN PEOPLE RISE – THE SOUTH MOLTON DECLARATION

"Anything that has been done legally can be undone legally." — RA

1. A DECLARATION OF THE SOVEREIGNTY OF THE PEOPLE

By the year 2001 it was clear to most of the British people that the democratic constitution of the United Kingdom had been virtually destroyed by those who swore they were preserving it. The Labour, Conservative and Liberal Democrat Parties had all claimed, (in stark contrast to the Morgan judgement quoted in the introduction to this book) that the United Kingdom, the powers of its parliament and its national self-governance still existed. The South Molton Declaration invited candidates of the major political parties at the 2001 general election to do no more than support a Bill in Parliament which would confirm this.

The Declaration was launched in the Devon town of South Molton on St George's Day (23rd April) 1999. The local MP, a Liberal Democrat, having stood at the general election on the principle of opposing the EURO, later embraced it — thus accepting the abolition of the Pound and the Bank of England. The MP had thereby shown not a change of political belief but a betrayal of *constitutional principle* (and hence the sovereignty of the people enshrined in that constitution) which all voters, regardless of party allegiance, had a right to take for granted.

When the absolute monarch ruled then that monarch was "sovereign". When over the centuries after Magna Carta in 1215, Parliament took more and more powers from the "sovereign" and in particular after the "Glorious Revolution" of 1688, Parliament (or "the King in Parliament") became the true sovereign power. But when the era of representative democracy dawned that sovereignty transferred not to members of Parliament but to those who elected them to sit in that parliament - the people. The sovereignty of the people is of course the very definition of democracy and yet this simple truth of all democratic constitutions has been either totally ignored or forgotten in the United Kingdom. Indeed in many of the new parliamentary systems of continental Europe these elementary truths were perhaps never learned in the first place and so their imposition of authoritarian rule and the transfer of that rule to Brussels and the European Central Bank, to bureaucrats and committees of ministers (in most cases without any reference to their electorates) came naturally to them.

So Parliament (which permitted Government ministers to misuse the anachronistic authoritarianism of the Crown Prerogative to sign European Treaties behind the backs of the people) is not sovereign. Government ministers are not sovereign. Even the Monarchy is not "sovereign". Each Parliament only *represents* the *true* sovereigns (the voters) for its statutory term — a maximum of five years. It is only when this elementary truth is grasped that the disgraceful actions of politicians in Britain and other once sovereign European nations become clear.

Those who have struggled over the last 30 years first to warn of the loss of our democratic rights and then to seek to restore those rights have made fundamental mistakes. They allowed the political agenda to be set by those who sought to bypass and then destroy the people's sovereignty and who used non-parliamentary methods (like international treaties) to disguise the fact. We therefore had to react against the proposals of others and were forced into the negative — saying "no" to our opponents' initiatives. Secondly we allowed important arguments about sovereignty, constitution and democracy *which are firm and inalienable principles* to be drowned by arguments about politics, trade and economics which are more open to interpretation and argument. We must never forget that liberal democracies can only enjoy their liberalism if they are protected by a structure of constitutional certainty. It is totalitarian and fascist regimes which thrive on uncertain and flexible structures, where parliament rapidly takes on authoritarian powers over the people and where the law is no longer a neutral defender of all but becomes an arbitrary tool of the State. Man is free only where he is ruled by laws made by those he can sack and within the security of a democratic constitution which *grants the right* to sack his lawmakers. Those who make laws must themselves be subject to the full vigour of those laws. Laws must always have general application and must never be targeted at particular groups, individuals or political parties. If men and not laws, rule then no man is free.

Although at first justified to promote public awareness those in Britain who resisted the new European tyranny continued too long to fight the "major" political parties only through *new* political parties, rather than through a direct appeal to the voters whose sovereign rights were being destroyed.

The South Molton Declaration requires a prospective candidate to *commit by his signature* to putting a bill before parliament which confirms the United Kingdom is a self-governing democratic nation with control of e.g. its borders, taxation, public spending, its own laws, its courts, the ability to sign international treaties etc. *The Declaration demands constitutional commitment, not political agreement. Indeed candidates signed up to the democratic nation which Labour, Liberal and Conservative Parties claimed we still possessed.* ("In Europe but not ruled by Europe" as William Hague said and a "patriotic nation" as Blair claimed). The Declaration is a contractual, moral and public commitment, the breaking of which (like the refusal to sign) will mean public exposure of individual parliamentary candidates. Who, in the long run, would vote for a parliamentary candidate who refuses to acknowledge the sovereignty of the voter — and hence the democratic rights of his own parliament and government?

Either candidates signed and became *"Declaration Candidates"* or by refusing to sign *they were admitting that they had already given away the pillars of a self governing nation (i.e. the United Kingdom no longer exists) and that they were refusing to do anything about it* — in which case they would be rejected by their electorates. The main aim was to maximise the number of Declaration Candidates and the number of *Declaration MPs* (on both sides of the House) in parliament. Unlike fighting through new political parties it was possible for all candidates to remain with their ideological roots and yet make this vital constitutional and democratic commitment to the sovereignty of the people.

The South Molton Declaration can be used as proof of the *real* platform of an MP should he/she refuse to sign. It can equally demonstrate the democratic and constitutional trustworthiness of those who *do* sign ("Declaration Candidates") thus boosting their electoral chances; and it can be used by those who sign *as a shield* against those disreputable parties which might otherwise stand against and help to defeat democratic and patriotic candidates.

The South Molton Declaration, as used at the 2001 British general election summed up the entire work and aims of the anti-fascist movement for free democratic nations in one clear, constitutionally powerful document. If two generations of politicians had lied to the people about their sovereign rights, then all legislation which had undermined the United Kingdom's constitutional rights to self-government would be automatically repealed. In other words that very process which destroyed British democracy (implied repeal of the critical pillars of our constitution) would be applied to *restoring* that constitution, the status of "being in Europe but not ruled by Europe" would be assured and the full intentions of the British Parliament in 1972 and the British people through the referendum in 1975 would be realised.

2. THE RESULTS OF AN OPINION POLL

The Opinion Research Company MORI conducted for the South Molton Declaration an opinion poll with a representative quota sample of 1,945 adults aged 18 plus at 189 sampling points across Britain between 22nd and 27th March 2001.

The following question was put:

"At the General Election all Labour, Conservative and Liberal Democrat candidates will be asked to sign the South Molton Declaration. The Declaration says that, if elected, they will put a Bill before parliament stating that only the British Parliament at Westminster should pass and repeal laws that affect the British people. This would in particular restrict the powers of the European Union over Britain."

If the . . . . (the name of the Party *which the respondent has already said he will vote for*) candidate refused to sign such a Declaration, which of these do you think you would be most likely to do?

THE RESULTS WERE AS FOLLOWS

FOR ALL VOTING:

A   I would vote for a different candidate who has signed the Declaration 30%

B   I would vote for the same candidate 47%

C   I would not vote. 12%

Don't know 11%

THIS MOST REMARKABLE RESULT SHOWS THAT 30% WOULD VOTE FOR A DIFFERENT CANDIDATE IF THEY DID NOT SIGN THE SOUTH MOLTON DECLARATION AND A FURTHER 12% WOULD TAKE THEIR VOTE FROM THEIR PREFERRED CANDIDATE AND NOT VOTE AT ALL.

IN OTHER WORDS 42% OF THE ELECTORATE WOULD SWITCH THEIR VOTE IF THEIR OWN PARTY'S CANDIDATE REFUSED TO SIGN THE SOUTH MOLTON DECLARATION.

THE EFFECT ON CONSERVATIVE VOTERS IS EVEN MORE REMARKABLE:

A   I would vote for a different candidate
     who has signed the Declaration 40%

B   I would vote for the same candiate 37%

C   I would not vote. 15%

Don't know 8%

IN OTHER WORDS 55% OF CONSERVATIVES WOULD CHANGE THEIR VOTE FROM THE CONSERVATIVE PARTY IF THEIR CANDIDATE DID NOT SIGN THE SOUTH MOLTON DECLARATION (OR PRESUMABLY A SIMILAR DOCUMENT WHICH HAD THE SAME EFFECT)

SOCIAL CLASS:

The highest percentage of those saying they would change their vote to a candidate who DID sign the South Molton Declaration was in the highest social classification AB — **33%**

REGIONS:

The highest percentage of voters saying they would change their vote to a candidate who DID sign the Declaration or to "would not vote" was in the North East Region of England — - **76%**

CONSERVATIVE YOUTH:

The most remarkable figure in the survey is the percentage of Conservative voters between 18 and 24 who say that they will switch their vote to another candidate or to "would not vote" if their Conservative candidate did not sign the Declaration - **72%!!**

EVEN IN THE LABOUR PARTY WITH A PRIME MINISTER WILLING TO ABOLISH THE POUND AND "POOL NATIONAL SOVEREIGNTY":

34% of Labour supporters would switch their vote (24% to a candidate who did sign and 10% to "would not vote") if their Labour candidate did not sign the South Molton Declaration.

THE LIBERAL DEMOCRAT PARTY

By far the most avid destroyers of national self governance are Liberal Democrat politicians — and indeed their voters would be the most loyal to their party candidate even if he did not sign the Declaration. **Nevertheless a total of 41% of Liberal Democrats would still switch their vote if their candidate did not sign the Declaration. 31% to a candidate who had signed and 10% to "would not vote". But in the North East of England no fewer than 69% of Liberal Democrats would switch to a candidate who had signed and of the younger Liberal Democrats (age 25-34) 40% would switch their vote, far more than Labour (25%) and Conservative (31%) in the same age group.**

3.   THE DECLARATION AT THE 2001 GENERAL ELECTION

Of the candidates who signed the South Molton Declaration the most successful received 18,000 votes, 48% of the total in his constituency and became the first Declaration MP. The three candidates who did the most advertising of the fact that they had signed (all Conservative) obtained swings to them of 5.9%,

6.1% and 4.1% (the average swing to Conservatives nation-wide was only 1.8%). Many Liberal Democrat candidates were intimidated by their party hierarchy who told them not to read the Declaration but "bin it". Conservative candidates were intimidated by Francis Maude MP, the Tories' Shadow Foreign Secretary who wrote three times to all Conservative candidates warning them against the Declaration. He was therefore effectively admitting that the Tory policy of 'In Europe but not ruled by Europe' was a complete fraud, *because 'not being ruled by Europe' was precisely what the South Molton Declaration expressed.*

The average number of votes cast for Declaration candidates was 10,886 and the average percentage of the vote in their constituencies was 26%. A number of candidates indicated that they would reconsider the Declaration after the election. It is of course never too late to sign and to take action by laying a Bill before parliament. The South Molton Declaration will continue in all parliamentary elections until the sovereignty of the British people and the power of their parliament is restored.

The South Molton Declaration was the subject of several mailings by the major parties to their candidates, the organisers corresponded with hundreds of candidates and provided the evidence (through the MORI Poll, see above) of the votes available to those who sign. The United Kingdom's most distinguished and internationally most admired former Prime Minister, Margaret Thatcher, wrote of the declaration:

> Thank you so much for your letter informing me about the South Molton Declaration. Ever since 1215 at Runnymede the English people have been asserting their sovereign rights. I am glad to see the same spirit is still alive and well in the British people almost 800 years later.

But most important of all the Declaration set the standard by which Britain's democratic nationhood and the sovereignty of the British people will one day be recovered. It provided the means by which candidates can remain with their traditional parties and yet make a principled constitutional stand and demonstrated that there is an alternative to the decadence of the "major" political parties (which, as in the 1930s, had betrayed everything they swore to uphold) on the one hand and on the other the extremism of those fringe parties which inevitably arise when the instincts of decent, moderate people are affronted. The Declaration sought to avoid the collapse into political extremism which has tempted desperate people in the past and it will live on for every future parliamentary election until the British people have restored their sovereignty, democracy and nationhood.

4. THE FUTURE OF DEMOCRATIC NATIONHOOD

At the 2001 British general election, at future elections in the United Kingdom and in other countries seeking to restore their democratic nationhood the South Molton Declaration can ensure that the voters elect only those candidates who commit to laying a bill before parliament affirming the essence of democracy — the sovereignty of the people.

The declaration allows those *who believe in* a nation's democracy to confront those who will be forced to admit publicly *that they do not.* The positive will be taken for granted, the opposition will be forced to say "No", and the defeat of such candidates will *permanently change* the composition of future parliaments. If a parliamentary candidate in any nation refuses to sign up to the sovereignty of the people then it is clear that democracy no longer exists. New representatives must therefore replace those who have betrayed that sovereignty.

Those who have deceived so many and destroyed so much by constitutional manipulation and by bypassing the sovereignty of the people must never be allowed to keep their ill-gotten gains. For, drunk as they are with their success, there is now no obnoxious enterprise of elitist corporatism and State arrogance of which they do not think themselves capable. Free peoples of all nations must rise up against this evil which has once again gone forth from the bowels of continental Europe, threatening to infest the whole world with its fascist creed.

5. THE TEXT OF THE SOUTH MOLTON DECLARATION

The Following is the text of the South Molton Declaration which will be the basis of a future Bill laid before Parliament, re-asserting the sovereignty of the British people and the powers of their parliament. The final drafting of a Bill may of course be different in expression, accommodating the best knowledge of parliamentary and constitutional law but the South Molton Bill — or a document of equivalent force — will one day re-assert those sovereign and parliamentary rights which 800 years of internal and external struggle have provided to a fortunate British people.

The South Molton Declaration
The Democratic Declaration of a prospective MP to the electorate.

I, ... hereby irrevocably Declare to my electorate that at the first opportunity following my election, I shall lay before Parliament and vote for a Bill, or vote in favour of such a Bill presented by others, (and continue to do so until the Bill is passed into law) which, in accordance with the rights of all peoples to self determination as enshrined in the United Nations Covenant on Civil and Political Rights of 1966:

Asserts the sole authority of the Westminster Parliament to initiate, pass and repeal all legislation and regulation applied to the people of the United Kingdom and asserts the supreme authority of the British judiciary in all law applied to the people of the United Kingdom

And recognizes:

* the sole allegiance of MPs, ministers and British officials to the Parliament and democratic institutions of the United

Kingdom and that all British subjects owe allegiance, duties and obligations only to the United Kingdom.

- the exclusive control by the Westminster Parliament over who resides within and votes in any elections in the United Kingdom, control over the borders of the United Kingdom and the exclusive right to grant or withhold permission to cross those borders.

- the historic rights of British subjects to *inter alia* Habeas Corpus, Trial by Jury and presumed innocence and prevents their extradition to any jurisdiction which does not afford such rights or which refuses to extradite to the United Kingdom.

- the sole control by the Bank of England of all British gold and foreign currency reserves (and their location within the United Kingdom) and Bank of England or British Government control over the Pound Sterling, British national monetary policy and interest rates.

- the right of the British Government, as the Representative of a Sovereign British people and nation, to sign international treaties and conventions which facilitate trade and co-operation between nations but which in no way compromise the supreme authority of the Parliament of the United Kingdom.

And I hereby pledge that I will vote against any legislation which explicitly or impliedly repeals or contravenes the above principles, so long as I remain a Member of Parliament.

I, ... being the . . . . prospective parliamentary candidate for . . . . hereby declare this . . . . . . day of . . . . 200 . . . that, should I not fulfil the terms of this Agreement at the first opportunity after being elected to Parliament, I will immediately resign so that a by-election may be held and a new Member elected to serve for the remainder of the parliament.

Signed . . . . Date: . . . .

CONCLUSION

Since the late 1980s I have continuously warned of a return to conditions, political motivations and power structures in Europe similar to those pertaining just before the first and second world wars. These warnings were expressed most fully in my book Europe's Full Circle first published in 1996. In the leaflet Yugoslavia and its Enemies, published in 1998 (reproduced in chapter 4 of this book) the parallels for the Yugoslavs were particularly striking. I am pleased to see that by the end of the 1990s a few brave analysts had at last begun to make the same point, most notably in John Laughland's recent book The Tainted Source. In the Spectator of 17th July 1999 Frank Johnson the distinguished historian and journalist wrote:

> So July of this century's last year finds British ministers concerned with the same subjects as in the July of what was really the previous century's last year — July 1914. That is, Serbia and Ireland.

I would add to that list Russia and the prospect in both periods of Slav Orthodoxy, outraged by the attacks on Serbia and the expansion of German Europe, marshalling resources to prepare for future conflict. Johnson in his 1999 article reminded his readers of the conflict in 1914 between the "navalists" and the "continentalists":

> Admittedly the latter differed from today's cominitted continentalists in that they wanted to oppose and if necessary go to war with Germany. Today's committed continentalists want to join with her in a new polity. But still Germany is at the heart of our problem.

I hope I have demonstrated in this book that through anti democratic means and skilful deception the peoples and na-

189

tional parliaments of Western Europe have unwittingly surrendered to a new continental European superpower (even the great deceiver Tony Blair calls it a "superpower not a superstate") all the characteristics of democratic nationhood and much of the rights of popular sovereignty for which millions of Europeans died in two world wars.

As a consequence the results of both world wars have been undone. The free nations established after the second world war are well on their way to utter destruction and the post first world war settlement has effectively been torn up by Germany which is re- establishing its hegemony in central and eastern Europe, using the tool of the European Union and its citizenship to re-assert economic and industrial power and ownership.

The methods whereby this has come about have been analysed and the chief beneficiaries of this process (German imperialism and continental fascism) have been described. There is no excuse for parliamentarians who passed the obnoxious legislation, for newspapers, radio and television who ignored the continuous destruction of democratic rights over many decades or so effectively censored the voices of protest.

Appendix II lists the names of the parliamentarians who were the main supporters of the treaties and legislation which have largely wiped out the democratic powers of the parliament which they swore by oath to defend. They are the usual mixture of "Liberal Democrat" corporatist capitalists, State interventionists in the Conservative Party and "Social Democrats", all of whom arrived at anti democratic corporatism in much the same way as their predecessors arrived at 1930s fascism — via "The Third Way". Those who emphasise the role of the State and "wise" government constantly look for ways to control the worst effects of their own economic and democratic distortions. They soon look to supranational controls to prevent free men escaping their depredations at the level of the nation state. Those who reject the organic systems of family, community, nation, the evolving common law and personal allegiance seek to replace them with corporate bodies which claim to "repre-

190

sent the people", committees, government appointed agencies, the State and the supranational state. Those who cannot tolerate competition between companies or between the people and the state cannot tolerate competition between nations. Those who seek to organise life on corporate lines cannot tolerate the sovereignty of electors and those who are building an empire cannot tolerate the freedom of nations to opt out of that empire.

There can be no better examples of the intolerance which proves the essentially fascist nature of the European Union than the treatment of the Danes when they voted no to the Maastricht Treaty and the contempt for the Irish when they resoundingly rejected the Nice Treaty. The frustration of German imperialism was expressed by Chancellor Gerhard Schroeder:

> "The enlargement process is irreversible. ... The Irish people's decision must be respected but it must not be allowed to hold up the process."

If the democratic voice of a nation cannot hold up a process then that process cannot be democratic. And indeed this is not the first time that German Europe has intervened to override national governments, using the power and force of "European integration" to get its own way. Countries applying to the European Union in the Balkans area were told by a German spokesman during the war against Yugoslavia that they must allow NATO troops and supplies to cross their territory — or lose their status as EU applicants. Germany threatened the USA with EU trade obstruction if the American Government did not stop litigation by Jews in the US courts against German businesses which had employed slave Labour during the war.

Recently the Czech Prime Minister said that the German EU Commissioner Gunter Verheugen (responsible for EU *enlargement* — a wonderful euphemism) had told him in private conversation that if Vaclav Klaus, the eurosceptic leader of the Czech opposition, came to power "the Czech Republic will not become a member of the European Union". That this was not merely an observation but a threat became clear when, confronted with this story by a journalist, Verheugen replied "I

191

would never say something like that in public." It was of course the manipulation of the other EU member states at the time of the negotiation of the Maastricht Treaty that allowed Germany to force through the recognition of Croatia by the EU. The list of demands and achievements of the German State is long and will not end until the once free and democratic nations of Europe retrieve their freedom.

All the good readers of this book need to ask themselves is a few straightforward questions about the European Union.

1. Why if the European Union is supposed to have prevented war in Europe did we need NATO at all? Seven years after the Maastricht Treaty the European Union has destroyed the national democracies of 15 countries, caused 17 million unemployed, threatened Norway, broken up Czechoslovakia, broken up Yugoslavia and attacked Britain's long time ally, Serbia. If that is preventing war most Europeans would hate to think what peace would be like.

2. Why if the Common Market, the European Community and now the European Union are supposed to have made us all richer are we not able to afford our separate national democracies something we *could* afford when we were poorer?

3. Why if Europe is democratic do we see the rise of ever more gigantic corporate monopolies which national parliaments always agreed were a threat to democracy? And why was war declared against Yugoslavia without any approval by the British parliament?

4. When research has repeatedly shown that gigantic corporations — even with the benefit of efficient market signals like prices, interest rates, exchange rates, profits etc — are less efficient than smaller companies how will gigantic political empires like the EU be more efficient democratically where communication between electors and elected is so much more difficult? Long term trends show how, as the European Union has gained ever more power, the numbers of people voting in

European and national elections has steadily, and recently dramatically declined.

5. Why if the EU is supposed to stop war in Europe have we lost far more of our nation, democracy and constitution today than we had at the depths of our misfortunes in the last war? **If war is no longer possible is it because it is no longer necessary?**

6. Why, when large multinational states like the Soviet Union have broken up in order to re-establish democracy is the european union doing the opposite? Why, when countries like Poland, Latvia, Lithuania and Czechoslovakia escaped from the anti democratic embrace of the Soviet Empire are they being asked to surrender their democratic nationhood and newly won parliamentary rights to the European Commission and the embrace of German Europe? It was The Prague Post, which noted that "Czechoslovakia has gone from being a soviet satellite to a German Protectorate".

7. Why, when democracy only arose after the establishment of nation-states, are we now abolishing nation states? At the recent British general election, in a country generally regarded as one of the most democratic in the world, only 59% of the population bothered to vote — the lowest level since the introduction of the universal franchise. If the British people no longer vote (because they see that power no longer resides in their parliament) then it is no wonder that few throughout the "European" Union bother to vote in European Parliament elections — for democratic accountability did not go there either. Rather it disappeared and real power is now exercised by the German State, big business, big unions, lobby groups and the European Commission and its appointees.

8. Why, if the evils of the European past are to be prevented in the future, are those very forces which brought about those evils so prominent in creating this new Europe and why are those who offered the greatest resistance (Czechoslovakia, Britain, Norway, Yugoslavia) now under such attack for resisting that new power?

Never have the United Kingdom in particular and the nations of Europe in general been in such peril. At least before and during previous wars the identity and intentions of the aggressors were clear long before they achieved their aims. Today most of those aims have been achieved without there being any real general consciousness of danger. If the first step towards redemption is an insight into the *opposite* of democracy, into the kind of people who seek to destroy us and the methods they use, then I hope this book might set the British and European peoples on the road to restoring democratic, free trading nationhood — the only hope for peace, not just in Europe but throughout the world.

APPENDIX I
EUROPEAN UNION PROPAGANDA IN BRITISH SCHOOLS

After the publication and distribution to schools of the "Partners in Europe" pack of pro European union propaganda and the (eventual) trashing of the European Commission's disgraceful "Strawberry Ice Cream War" (targeted at schoolchildren and described by the left as racist and by the right as an attack on democratic nations) we now have yet another "information" brochure from the European Union — "EUROQUEST".

Like the other pro European Union propaganda publications of the Labour Government and the European Union, Euroquest is a glossy brochure distributed to schools in the name of "information" but which of course blatantly defies the Education Act's prohibition of politically biased material in schools. The Department for Education itself has stated in the past that in the 1996 Education Act (as in previous versions):

> "Section 406 of the Act requires school governing bodies, headteachers and local authorities to forbid the promotion of partisan political views in the teaching of any subject in schools .... Section 407 requires them to take all reasonable practical steps to ensure that where political or controversial issues are brought to pupils attention they are offered a balanced resentation of opposing views."

But such rules apparently do not apply to the European Commission in its various guises:

The UK Representation of the European Commission

The UK Office of the European Parliament

Relay Europe Ltd

The Charlemagne Group of Companies

The European Movement

European Resource Centres for Schools and Colleges (organised in British Regions)

The Directorate for European Operations at the Open University

Regional "Euro-Forums" (Run by the British Government giving "information" about for example, the EURO)

"Euroquest" is their latest venture into the "education" of our children about the obvious(!) advantages of sacrificing our nation, parliament and democracy on the altar of the European Union.

The publication begins by describing itself as "a travellers guide" a "trail of questions and answers about the European Union". On the first page it uses interchangeably and without definition "the European Union" and "Europe". The latter of course only consists of 15 countries whose national democratic parliaments have been destroyed in favour of a supranational bureaucracy in Brussels. The latter consists of 42 countries, 27 of which are still democratic nations, including the two richest, Norway and Switzerland which have repeatedly voted against joining the "European Union". But there is of course a severe limit to the "educational" remit of the European Commission's latest publication !

On a map of "Europe" there are no names given for Switzerland, Norway and Yugoslavia — they are "non countries"! In lauding the potential expansion of the European Union (ie the destruction of the democratic national constitutions of those countries which might enter) the pretence is precisely the opposite to that "ever closer, political intergration" which "European" Union leaders propagate within the EU. They merely assert:

> The bigger the EU becomes the more people there would be to sell to and more good ideas to share from all the different countries.

In other words to our schoolchildren they repeat the same lies and deception as in 1972 when Britons were told they were joining a "Common Market" of sovereign self-governing, free trading nations. Then as now of course the reality was different from the propaganda.

This touchy-feely, innocuous description of the EU is the watchword throughout this propaganda publication: "The European Union is like a club" when of course it is nothing of the sort. It is a superstate based on a constitution which binds its members in virtually every aspect of political, economic, budgetary and now increasingly foreign and defence policy. And it does so, as the European Treaties repeat *ad nauseam* "irrevocably and irreversibly". Indeed there is no procedure for withdrawal — not quite the kind of "club" most of us would wish to join.

> The Club was started after the Second World War to make sure that there are no more wars between the countries of Europe.

Of course the European Common Market — with only 6 members — was not founded until 1957. It was NATO, the North Atlantic Treaty Organisation (which even today has far more members than the EU) which preserved the peace in Europe. Only 7 years after the Maastricht Treaty gave even more powers to the European Union and turned all nationals into "European citizens", we have war in Europe. The Yugoslav war was started in 1989 with the recognition of Croatia by Germany and the European Union and the break up of Yugoslavia, a recognised sovereign nation. This was an exact repeat of the maneuvers of Germany prior to the first and second world wars.

"Euroquest" goes on to claim that "all members of the EU pay a membership fee and this money is used to help everybody". In fact Britain is the second largest contributor to the budget and when Euroflags are put up outside some industrial or infrastrcuture projects in Britain claiming that the EU has "funded" it, this is a lie. Britain gets no money from the EU, it only — occasionally — gets back a small proportion of what British taxpayers have contributed. Even that depends on our doing what Brussels, not our own parliament, decides is best for us.

YOUR PASSPORT: On page two of "Euroquest" there is a picture of a British passport, under the caption "this is an EU passport, it proves you are a citizen of the European Union". This is of course what British politicians have always denied — that it doesn't mean "citizenship" in the strict sense of the word! But in fact it is designed to mean just that. The Maastricht Treaty makes it clear that we have "duties and obligations" towards this European Union of which — without our consent — we have been made "citizens". Indeed the "corpus juris" proposed by the European Union is the latest attempt to combat fraud (caused of course by its own agricultural policy) and it relies on this "citizenship" to argue for the takeover of national legal systems by the EU!

One of the favourite tricks of those political institutions (and empires) who seek to enhance their reputation and demonstrate how we cannot do without them is to attach themselves to projects and ideas which were well established and ran perfectly well without their "help". In "Euroquest" the European Union claims that "agreements between countries are making it easier and safer for people to travel around the European Union". But of course such agreements were made long before the European Union existed and such agreements are made between countries which are not in the European Union, and between EU members and non members.

The document also claims that the EU "has helped to build new bridges, tunnels and high speed railways". This is nonsense — the EU has merely attached its name to certain projects either by simply lending money (at normal commercial rates) or returning some of the taxes it has extracted from member nations (without any of the democratic processes usual within the national parliaments).

INTERNATIONAL TRADE: In another section "Euroquest" claims

> We can buy things from all 15 countries without paying the extra costs or duty usually put on things bought from other countries.

This is of course the success not of the EU but of the World Trade Organisation which has dismantled many barriers to free trade in recent years — and on a global basis, not just for a few countries in Europe. Secondly this "free trade" does not apply to the majority of European countries (27 of them) which are outside the EU. In particular the poor countries of eastern Europe are faced with very high tariff barriers for their exports to the EU.

INTERNATIONAL POLLUTION: The brochure further claims that: "The EU countries have agreed to help reduce air pollution." In fact many EU countries are being allowed to increase air pollution while the UK itself has reduced pollution drastically in recent years. In any case there is no point in reducing air pollution for some countries in a small part of Europe if others refuse to do the same. That is why there are world agreements (as in the Kyoto summit) to tackle air and sea pollution which are more relevant than the EU's parochial attempts.

In another section the brochure claims that the EU "sets high standards for our waste water". In fact the most polluted waters in Europe flow through the EU's own "capital" — Brussels — where untreated sewerage eventually flows into the sea at the aptly named "Flushing". The brochure refers to sea, river and air pollution saying that they "know no frontiers". But that has always been the case and international agreements between sovereign self governing nations have always covered such matters. Indeed if we accepted the EU's argument (that pollution knows no frontiers therefore national frontiers should not exist) then the EU itself should not exist since it has artificial frontiers which cannot stop pollution (not least with a non member Switzerland right in the middle of Europe!)

FOOTBALL PROPAGANDA: In a populist attempt to link the EU's propaganda to football, "Euroquest" lists well known European football teams (Ajax, Manchester United, Barcelona etc). "Sport offers a chance for people from different countries to meet and get to know each other", says "Euroquest". But strangely the children are not encouraged to get to know about teams from Moscow or Warsaw or Zurich or Oslo! These are of course teams from the free, democratic nations of Europe, not from the European Union.

WHAT IS EUROPE? In another section of the brochure in the usual "Further activities" for students the pupils are encouraged to "make contact with someone who was born in another EU country" — but not of course anyone born in Norway or Switzerland or Yugoslavia or Poland, or Czechoslovakia! It would be interesting to hear the response of a teacher whose pupil asks why her friend from Norway is not "European". That might just prove the blatantly politicised nature of this brochure. It would be clear that it is not an exercise in education about internationalism and the countries of Europe but a propaganda exercise on behalf of the new EU superstate.

ABOLISHING THE POUND: The propaganda of course includes a section on the EURO the purpose of which, students are told, is to "make it much easier to travel, to shop or to open a bank account in any of the 15 countries". There is no mention that 3 of the 15 EU countries have opted out of the EURO. There is no mention of the fact that the single currency abolishes the national currencies, national central banks and of course the key attribute of national sovereignty (a national treasury and democratic control over monetary and fiscal affairs).

Euroquest claims that different currencies "make it more expensive to buy and sell between members states" but the main differences in costs are national taxes, bureaucracy, transportation, social and employment costs, government subsidies and state protection of its own industries. And if the costs of trade are so high outside the EURO why are French and German companies investing so heavily in Britain?

FARMING AND FISHING: On page 11 of the brochure "Farming and fishing in the European Union" is described. The page is devoted to Denmark which "catches the most fish" — much of it of course from British territorial waters which, thanks to the Treaty of Rome, the European Union took away from Britain and turned into "Community" fishing grounds.

Farmers, the students are told "are paid to help them grow crops to feed all the people in the EU". Needless to say they don't mention that millions of pounds are spent paying farmers *not* to grow anything at all and that Britain for instance is not allowed to produce more than 70% of its own milk (even though we used to be self sufficient in milk).

They even have the nerve to say that the "EU encourages farmers to use fewer chemicals to reduce the damage to the environment" when of course the principal characteristic of the European Union's farming policy is to buy everything farmers produce at a fixed price thus encouraging them to farm ever more intensively and to produce (using more fertiliser) as much as possible from every acre of land.

The EU claims it is "controlling the number of fish taken from the sea". In fact the farcical fish quota system means that hundreds of thousands of tons of dead fish are thrown back into the sea because the foolish fish that swim into the nets do not realise that the EU does not want them to be caught! The massive waste — and pollution — caused by this disgraceful policy is recognised throughout the world as the worst man-made scandal in the history of fishing.

The United Nations recently produced a report which showed that the best fish preservation scheme was run by the Falkland Islands — the only place where the British Government actually controls its own fishing grounds!

But dumping dead fish at sea is not the only dumping done by the European Union. It also dumps (i.e. offloads at low prices) its excess agricultural and fish products on third word countries, where very poor local farmers and fishermen are put out of business.

POLITICISING RESEARCH AND DEVELOPMENT: On page 12 of the brochure "Research and Development in the European Union" is discussed: "The EU countries are working together on scientific projects and research". What they don't say is that British scientists who work, as they traditionally have done, with colleagues in the USA, Australia or Canada for instance do not get any EU funding. If they want funds they have to work with Italians, Germans or other EU "citizens". This is of course a direct tax on successful British research and a subsidy to exclusively EU research bodies.

TRADE: The brochure is not averse to downright lies. It claims that "59% of UK exports are sold to EU countries". In fact taking away "entrepot trade" (ie goods which go to Antwerp or Rotterdam first on their way to eg the USA or Australia) and including, as we must, all trade in services and finance as well as goods, we export about 40% to the other EU countries. But this trade is and always has been massively negative - i.e. we have a large balance of payments deficit which has now reached a cumulative 150,000m since we joined the European Common Market in 1973.

Needless to say a large volume of trade with one country (never mind a group of countries) does not mean you have to surrender your democratic self government to that trading partner. On that basis Canada and probably Mexico would long ago have become part of the United States and most of the former Soviet satellite countries would have rejoined the Soviet Union.

ORGANISED CELEBRATION: In pursuit of the fundamentally political aims of "Euroquest" students are asked to celebrate "Europe Day" which commemorates "the day in 1950 when the idea of a united Europe was first thought of". Of course it was thought of long before that — by Hitler and the Nazis and by Napoleon and in slightly more modest proportions by the bloodthirsty Charlemagne in the 8th century. But such antecedents must not be mentioned (although Charlemagne, having lived 1200 years ago and safely thought to have been forgotten) features in much EU propaganda (the Charlemagne Prize, the EU's "Charlemagne House" in Hove etc).

THE "EUROPEAN PARLIAMENT": But there are some ideas about the EU which even this propaganda brochure dare not claim — that for instance the European Parliament is a parliament. Instead they say its role is "to give advice and help agree laws". On the same page the brochure describes the European Court as a "referee in any argument over EU laws". In fact of course like most courts its interpretations *make* the law. Indeed because the many European Treaties signed by 15 nations could only be agreed with the vaguest and least defined language, the European Court is constantly called upon to create law. It does so, on its own admission, not as an objective arbiter, but as a tool in the process of promoting the integration of the European Union.

THE "REGIONAL PRINCIPLE": One of the EU's principal methods of undermining the nation states and their parliaments and centering power in Brussels is the construction of "regions" which report directly to the EU, bypassing those national parliaments. (One of Hitler's ideas for destroying national governments). At the end of the brochure, under "further activities" students are encouraged to "write a letter to your MEP ... if there is something in your area (an interesting term!) you think should be changed". Why should they not write to their MP ? — because that might suggest that the European Union is irrelevant and that national parliaments and MPs still have validity.

In short this latest attempt to indoctrinate schoolchildren in the European Union's project of eliminating the sovereign democratic countries of Europe is a truly obnoxious propaganda which must be countered at all costs. Parents of schoolchildren must stop and refute this EU propaganda which is illegally circulating in our schools.

APPENDIX II

The major eurofederalist supporters among politicians, companies and organisations in Britain

POLITICIANS

Edward Heath (Prime Minister who removed the Sovereignty of the British people by Accession to the Treaty of Rome, Bilderberg attendee)

Robert Walter MP, North Dorset (long time activist for and former President of the European Movement who at every election claims he is a "eurosceptic")

Robin Cook MP

Tony Blair MP

Peter Mandelson MP

Dawn Primarolo MP

Kenneth Clarke MP

John Gummer MP

Ian Taylor MP

Menzies Campbell MP

Quentin Davies MP (When lunching at public expense in Brussels sent back a £55 botttle of wine "the bouquet is not quite right")

Anne MacKintosh MP (criticised by her constituents for being both an MP *and* an MEP)

Dennis McShane MP

Charles Kennedy MP

Stephen Byers MP

Tony Baldry MP ("would not the best memorial to the victims of Nazism be to create an enlarged European Union that extends to the countries of the Balkans and eastern Europe?")

David Curry MP

Peter Luff MP, Mid Worcestershire

Peter Bottomley MP

Damien Green MP

Chris Patten ex MP

John Butterfil MP

Anthony Nelson MP

Shaun Woodward ex Tory now Lab MP

David Atkinson MP (Member of "Parliamentary Group for World Government"!)

Anthony Steen MP

Michael Jack MP (Tory supporter of the Common Agricultural Policy)

Sir George Young MP

Jacqui Lait MP (Member of the pro EU Action Centre for Europe)

James Paice MP ("The EU must run British agriculture" "Fortunately we have seen off our smaller farmers in this country")

Allen Rogers MP (also "Parliamentary Group for World Government"!)

Joan Walley MP (also "Parliamentary Group for World Government"!)

Elliot Morley MP (Labour minister who thinks he is responsible for agriculture. Will not withdraw from CAP which would make him in charge of agriculture!)

OUTSIDE THE HOUSE OF COMMONS

Lord (Leon) Brittan (ex EU Commissioner, substantial pension)

Lord Marshall (Director British Airways, brought in ludicrous tailfin paintings)

Paddy Ashdown ex MP ("I don't expect the nation state to survive")

John Stevens ex Tory MEP, UK Representative of the Pan European Union

Lord Jenkins of Hillhead (former EU Commissioner, substantial EU pension)

Sir Roy Denman, former EU "Ambassador" (thinks Britain should have made peace with Hitler)

Lord Levene, Chairman, Deutsche Bank, said London would benefit from Euro membership)

Lord Hollick, Leading light in "Britain in Europe", close to Blair, turned Daily Express into europhile newspaper, it became loss making, sold it to a publisher of pornography

Pauline Green Labour MEP (Leader of Labour MEPs, close to now sacked Jacques Santer, president of the European Commission. Resisted taking action against the Commission despite van Buitenen evidence of corruption)

Roy Perry MEP Conservative ("When history is written the greatest achievement of the 20th century will be seen to be the creation of the EU")

Andrew Duff MEP Liberal Democrat

Lord Simon of Highbury (Director BP)

Baroness Nicholson of Winterbourne (Lib Dem, ex Conservative)

Lord Tugendhat (Director of a Building Society, suggested the Government should help pay off people's mortgages — i.e. pay off the buildings societies bad debts!)

Lord Hurd ("This is hardly a battleground of principle — which is a relief to those of us who were never enthusiastic about the single currency" — but he signed the Maastricht Treaty on Economic and Monetary Union)

Lord Howe (From his drafting with Heath of the original legislation in 1970/71 to his sabotage of Margaret Thatcher, a true believer in the European State)

Helmut Mauncher (Head of Nestle which owns Rowntrees, Chair of the europhile "European Round Table of Industrialists")

Adair Turner (ex Foreign Office, ex CBI)

Eluned Morgan MEP (refused to vote against corrupt European Commission)

Stephen Woodard (Director European Movement)

Hugh Dykes ex MP

Roger Evans ex MP Monmouth, **Peter Atkinson MP** Hexham (both promised Eurosceptic politics to their electorates and then repeatedly did the opposite in Parliament)

Edwina Currie ex Tory MP and BBC broadcaster (We could not ban "dangerous" British beef in the home market "because it would make the EU too unpopular")

Peter Luff (*not* the Tory MP of the same name, former Director European Movement, then Royal Commonwealth Society)
Tristan Garel Jones (ex Tory Foreign Office Minister, eurofanatic too weak a word!)
Peter Temple Morris (won Tory seat, switched to Labour, stood down at 2001 election)
Ron Davies (ex Labour MP — resigned as minister — sex scandal)
Sir Peter Emery ex Tory MP (ousted by his constituents)
Margaret Daly (Conservative ex MEP)
Brendan Donnelly ex Cons MEP ("Opposition to the Euro politically and economically unwise")
Tom Spencer ex MEP, (Resigned — caught smuggling pornography)
David Ashby ex MP
Maurice Fraser (Britain in Europe, adviser to Douglas Hurd)
Martin Bell ex MP (accused Neil Hamilton of corruption for receiving payments from al Fayed but refused to investigate Bilderberg Group for paying for hotel and flights for Blair, Brown, Kenneth Clarke etc)
John Tomlinson MEP

ORGANISATIONS

The European Movement (see leaflet published by Compuprint Publishing)
The Federal Trust
The Federal Trust Round Table
Confederation of British Industry (has manipulated results of polls of business opinion on Europe)
Action Centre for Europe
European Policy Forum
Centre for European Reform
Young European Movement
Young European Federalists
Joseph Rowntree Charitable Trust
Joseph Rowntree Reform Trust (deliberately *not* a charity in order to promote its political agenda)

The BBC (advertised in "Britain and Europe" publication, little pretence at objectivity in its broadcasting, aping its own appeasement of the 1930s)
Relay Europe Ltd and **The Charlemagne Group** of Companies! (Help to promote European Union propaganda during British parliamentary elections)
European Resource Centres for Schools and Colleges (organised in the regions)
The Directorate for European Operations at the **Open University**

CORPORATIONS

Toyota (Attacked its rival Land Rover and the Queen in an advert for Toyota cars: "Don't worry Your Majesty you're not the only British export which has had its day")
Sainsbury's
Marks and Spencer
Mitsubishi
BAT (Bilderberg supporter, found to be exploiting tobacco smuggling — Channel Four news report)
BMW
British Telecom
Unilever (Bilderberg founder, persistent propagandist for EU and Euro)
Barclays Bank (Member of Association for European Monetary Union)
Royal Bank of Scotland (now includes NatWest Bank, a founder member of the of the Association for Monetary Union in Europe)
British Aeropsace (Chief Executive said "Euro inevitable regardless of what politicians say — a classic fascist approach to democracy!)
Coopers & Lybrand
Unigate
Northern Foods (Director, Lord Haskins, close to Blair)
Anderson Consulting
Nissan

APPENDIX III

THE ANTI-DEMOCRATIC NATURE OF BLAIR'S "REGIONAL CONSTITUTIONAL CONVENTIONS'""

An attendee at the South West Constitutional Convention on 19th May 2001 wrote:

"I attended the Convention, with some difficulty, after being assured by the Bishop of Exeter that all views for and against would be welcome. This was a joke. It was obvious from the start that the purpose of the convention was to rubber stamp the call for an elected Assembly. The speakers included 6 Labour, 4 Liberal Democrats (one an MEP), 2 Greens and one Conservative (who had been a member of the EU's Committee of the Regions since 1993). Opponents of an elected Assembly had to make their objections from the floor, having no speaker from the platform and they were heckled and shouted down by the Labour and Liberal-Democrats who had been invited by their parties. Despite this, opponents of the idea seemed to outnumber the others and a special workshop had to be convened on the subject of the link between the EU and the Assemblies.

All speakers (except one) denied any links with Brussels even though the "South West Assembly" has its own "embassy" there! I challenged Cllr Chester Long, Chair of the South West Regional Assembly, to explain why, if there was no link, his predecessor, Chris Clarke and the Chairman of the Regional Development Agency Sir Michael Lickiss had gone to Brussels to dine EU officials in order to get their approval for the South West Regional strategic plans. We have a video of this Brussels meeting which was reported on the BBC and yet Cllr Long denied any knowledge of EU connections.

The one exception was a Stefaan De Rynck, a Belgian who was a member of the European Commission Governance Team, a responsibility of the European Commissioner for the Regions. He informed us that the Commission was working on a White Paper for the governance of the regions. He also said we should look for like regions on the continent so that we could form euro-zones (This has already happened in Kent and East Sussex). He received huge applause for his honesty but the rest still denied any EU involvement.

Before the Convention the supporters of a South West Assembly had issued a press release with 100 names of those who wanted an elected assembly. During the morning session I handed the Bishop of Exeter letters from 199 people (including journalists, a JP, an MP and a former Bishop) who opposed an Assembly. I asked the Bishop to enter this into the proceedings so that it could appear in the minutes. At the end of the seminar this petition still lay in the same position in front of the Bishop where I had placed it. He did not mention it but I once again insisted it be entered in the minutes. By this time many opponents of the Assembly had gone home. However we did force a vote (which the Bishop tried desperately to prevent) and the verdict was 83-52 for an Assembly. Had the petitions of both sides been included then the overall result would have been 252 to 183 against an assembly. I have now been informed that minutes of the meeting will not be available until September when they will be "launched" in book form (and at the taxpayers expense) to universities, colleges libraries etc - launched before anyone has a chance to check the contents. Although the organiser Mary Southcott, a Labour candidate, had the addresses of all those who attended she subsequently wrote only to supporters of the assembly saying how successful the day had been!"

Another meeting was held on 13th July to rubber stamp an elected assembly. An attendee reported the following:

"Those who opposed the regional system of Government outnumbered those for. However all those present were asked to sign a form saying they wanted an elected assembly. Those who refused to sign were asked to leave the meeting but they refused. The meeting was adjourned and they were again asked to leave but as it was a public meeting they remained seated. The Committee then decided to close the meeting and reconvene in another room away from the dissenters, which they did.

Guards were put on the doors to stop the public getting into this "public" meeting. Strangely, although expected, the Bishop of Exeter did not appear to chair the meeting."

When a similar convention was later organised in the West Midlands there was no plenary discussion and the attendees were split up into discussion groups, selected and chaired by those appointed by the organisers. Admission was by ticket only but unless the public happened to know about the event they could not apply for tickets. No votes were taken!

TO THE READER OF THIS BOOK

The British people have lost much of their nationhood and parliamentary and individual rights because those who have revealed those losses as they were occurring suffered severe censorship. It is precisely the kind of corporatist system which can remove the rights of a sovereign people behind their backs and hand over power to a supranational bureaucratic elite that has the power to censor or marginalise those who expose uncomfortable truths.

When a hideous truth is told (that the same European powers who were defeated in two world wars have created a system of constitutional deceit and achieved through "peaceful" methods what they failed to achieve through military means) then the teller is rarely believed. Indeed the more evil and fantastic the strategy he reveals, the easier it is for the architects of that strategy to attack him. The fact that most of those who have implemented these policies are ignorant of what they have done shows how critical is the education process of which this book is a small part.

But while this author has indeed suffered such censorship and such attacks from the corrupt political establishments who have destroyed the constitutional sovereignty of the British people, the people themselves have continued to read and buy in their thousands books like this.

We therefore appeal to you to ensure that this book is stocked in your local library, that friends and relations, local and national journalists and your political representatives are made aware of the grave message within these pages and that you turn the lessons you have learned into real democratic action within and outside your own political party or campaigning group. The "New World Order" and the corporatist European elite spend hundreds of millions of pounds every year on "information" at your expense. We hope you will help to turn this book into a powerful counter to these anti-democratic forces.

The Author

RODNEY ATKINSON BA MSC MIL

Rodney Atkinson is one of Britain's leading political economists, an expert on the constitutional effects of British membership of the European Union and a former adviser to ministers. He has a track record of successful prediction of economic and political crisis, having predicted in advance *inter alia* the collapse of oil prices in 1983, the fall in British house prices in 1989 and the end of the European Exchange Rate Mechanism in 1990. He has been a successful linguist and linguistic theorist, was formerly a lecturer at the University of Mainz, Germany and a merchant banker in the City of London. He is Chairman of Heritage Media Ltd, a regular supplier of programming to radio stations and proprietor of his own commercial property company.

He is the author of some 80 articles and policy papers and five internationally praised books on political economy: *Government against the People* (1986), *The Emancipated Society* (1988), *The Failure of the State* (1989) and on the European Union, *Treason at Maastricht* (with Norris McWhirter, fourth edition 1998) and *Europe's Full Circle* (third edition 1998, also published in Yugoslavia and Poland). For the lavish all party praise of these books see the author's website freenations.freeuk.com

He was Referendum Party candidate in North West Durham in the 1997 General Election (5.2% of the vote) and the lead UK Independence Party candidate for the North East Region in the 1999 European Elections (8.83% of the vote). He has been a contributor to radio and television programmes on both sides of the Atlantic. He launched the cross party South Molton Declaration in 1999.

INDEX

OTHER BOOKS BY RODNEY ATKINSON

EUROPE'S FULL CIRCLE
ISBN 0 9525110 3 7   1998   £10.00

First published in October 1996 (third edition December 1998) the book exposes the individuals and groups behind the secret plans for a European Super-State and the abolition of national democracies. Corporatist Europe has built its "Union" on the Nazi plan of 1942 supported then as now by Establishment figures and corporatist elites in Britain, Europe and the USA. Identical methods used by Hitler to rule Germany have been used to impose European Union rule on Britain and other nations. By 1999 15 nations' constitutions have been destroyed, eleven currencies and national banks have been abolished, a non democratic managerial class in Brussels rules Europe, Germany has been united, Czechoslovakia and Yugoslavia broken up and war declared on Serbia. 1930s appeasers and 1990s Euro-fascists compared. British industry attacks UK sovereignty. The secretive Bilderberg Group, its founders and influence. Censorship of criticism of the European Union in Britain.

"Records in convincing, sombre and well researched detail the destruction of the nation state. All who cherish our heritage should buy this book." — **Sir Louis Le Bailly, former Director General, Defence Intelligence Staff.**

"In this 160 page work there is so much that has not before been made public that it is a monument to past stealth." — **Norris McWhirter CBE**

"I like *Europe's Full Circle* a lot and will certainly talk about the book widely." — **Sir James Goldsmith**

"Congratulations on the sheer intellectual quality of the content, the depth of research and the most enjoyable style of writing." — **Sir James McKinnon**

"I congratulate you on putting together such a readable account of the way in which a 'new' fascism is creeping through Europe powered by corporatist elites through the European Union — their chosen instrument for attaining aims which we believed had been defeated in 1945." — **Lord Stoddart of Swindon (Labour)**

"It is to Rodney Atkinson, a brilliant pro-nation activist, that we owe the decisive insight on the delegation of general powers which is at the root of Britain's malaise." — *International Currency Review.*

"A real tour de force" — **Andrew Roberts, author** *Eminent Churchillians.*

"Atkinson's awareness of the current dangers of the entire Maastricht project is timely and well developed An enlightening study." — *The Morning Star*

"Thanks for *Europe's Full Circle.* You are making a point that much needs making. The only downside to the military defeat of fascism was that people thought its ideas had gone away. I stand corrected on 'private enterprise' — 'Corporatist capitalism' shall be part of my lexicon henceforth." — **P. J. O'Rourke**

"Atkinson's book brilliantly illustrates the mortal danger of the EU ethos which reduces politics to managerial efficiency at the expense of democracy." — **Ian Milne,** *Eurofacts*

"The author has done a superb job in seeking to alert literate people to the colossal and dangerous impudence of corporate power which has already emasculated elected national legislatures." — *Fourth World Review*

"Absolutely first class." — **Sir Julian Hodge K.StG. K.St.J LLD**

"I am fascinated with your book Europe's Full Circle. Beautifully written and quite startling in its information." — **Cav Uff Robert Rietti OMRI**

TREASON AT MAASTRICHT
The destruction of the Nation State
Rodney Atkinson   Norris McWhirter
Second Edition Fourth Reprint   £10.00 paperback

Second revised and expanded edition, 1995. The first book to expose in detail the destructive effect of the Maastricht Treaty on the 800 year old British constitution. Describes the treason cases taken by the authors against Douglas Hurd and Francis Maude in the British courts and the response of the Crown Prosecution Service. The violation of the Queen's Coronation Oath. The overturning of inter alia Magna Carta, the Act of Settlement, the Union with Scotland Act, the 1795 Treason Act and significant case law from 1820 and 1932. Churchill on "Europe". How British European Commissioners violate their oath of allegiance to the Queen. Germany's invalid ratification of the Maastricht Treaty. A detailed comparison with the constitution of the USA and the cause of the American civil war. The Nazi origins of the European Union. Federalism and Conservative MEPs.

""In our fight for freedom your book was a cruise missile which I hope is still finding targets." — **Vice Admiral Sir Louis Le Bailly, former Director General, Defence Intelligence Staff**

"British Commissioners in Brussels should bear allegiance to one or other but not both sovereigns." — **Former Lord of Appeal in Ordinary and Master of the Rolls Lord Denning**

"Two latter day St Georges slashing to pieces the myths and lies woven around 'Europe'." — *This England* **Magazine**

"I agree and have bought more copies to circulate among other judges." — **High Court Judge**

"Many Australians, not only the ex British citizens, would find this book extremely enlightening ... a damning indictment of the Maastricht Treaty, exposing the Constitutional outrage which has already been committed." — **UK Settlers Association, Australia**

OTHER PUBLICATIONS
FROM THE PUBLISHER

Leaflets at £1 each or £6 for 100

The Euro — what it really means
Britain and Europe — the facts
Yugoslavia and its Enemies 1903-1999
European Union Propaganda in British Schools
15 Lies from the European Movement

Leaflets and books (add £1 per book) by post from
Compuprint Publishing
1 Sands Road
Swalwell
Newcastle upon Tyne NE16 3DJ